T0311552

Being, Becoming and Thriving as an Early Years Practitioner

Being, Becoming and Thriving as an Early Years Practitioner captures the authentic and often humorous experiences that occur when working with young children, providing a comprehensive and accessible guide to the reality of early years practice. Designed to support practitioners through the early stages of their careers, it reveals what child development theory looks like in practice through real-life examples and case studies alongside guidance on practitioner well-being, continuous professional development (CPD), and studying alongside work.

The book is structured around three key themes: **BEING, BECOMING,** and **THRIVING.** Each theme is divided into several chapters, and they cover a range of topics which will support you on your academic and professional journey including:

- Being a reflective practitioner
- Inclusion
- Key theorists
- Creativity
- The foundations of Play
- Reflection and Reflective Practice
- Continuous professional development

Aligned to some of the core components for Early Years and Education, the book blends theory and practice with humour and honesty, revealing what makes the Early Years such a magical sector in which to work. Including tools and activities to support your professional and academic journey, this is an essential read for any early years student beginning their Early Years journey.

Annie Pendrey is an educational consultant, lecturer, and creative researcher. Annie is studying for her PhD and is the author of *The Little Book of Reflective Practice* and *Reflection and Reflective Spaces in the Early Years*.

Being, Becoming and Thriving as an Early Years Practitioner

A Guide for Education and Early Years Students and Tutors

Annie Pendrey

Routledge
Taylor & Francis Group

LONDON AND NEW YORK

Designed cover image: © Getty Images

First published 2024
by Routledge
4 Park Square, Milton Park, Abingdon, Oxon, OX14 4RN

and by Routledge
605 Third Avenue, New York, NY 10158

Routledge is an imprint of the Taylor & Francis Group, an informa business

© 2024 Annie Pendrey

British Library Cataloguing-in-Publication Data
A catalogue record for this book is available from the British Library

ISBN: 978-1-032-42158-2 (hbk)
ISBN: 978-1-032-42151-3 (pbk)
ISBN: 978-1-003-36144-2 (ebk)

DOI: 10.4324/9781003361442

Typeset in Minion Pro
by KnowledgeWorks Global Ltd.

Contents

Contents

Theme – **BECOMING**   **65**

Theme – **THRIVING**   **125**

Contents

Acknowledgements

Without connections and communities of practice, I would not be able to write and share my gifts and experiences with you. My one connection, Lisa Broome, deserves a special thank you as she shares her professional practice with me daily and has contributed to this book with images and reflective accounts. Thank you, Lisa.

Another mention must go to my social media followers who continuously support me and my ideas. These people often pop into my message box with words of encouragement and even tell me if I have made a spelling mistake. These special people know who they are, and I thank you.

None of my words would be shared with you without the support of my family and I am going to dedicate this book to my husband who has supported me throughout my writing. There have been many times over the last few years when I have only shiny buttons in my purse and no money at all, but with his kindness and generosity, he has given me the platform to use my imagination and spread my creative wings.

My final thanks go to YOU, for picking up this book and beginning to interact with our words that we have chosen wisely from all our years of Early Years professional practice.

Introduction

Beginning Your Journey

Starting any new experience can be filled with a mixture of anxiety, trepidation, and excitement. As a NNEB to established author, I am always appreciative of anyone who chooses to read my words. So, thank you for choosing to pick up this book, which I hope will support you in your studies and/or professional practice. This is a book that combines my many years of Early Years practice and my teaching career from Early Years to Higher Education.

As you begin to make a start to read, interact, and reflect upon the contents of this book, I hope you will find its contents useful and applicable to your academic and professional studies. I hope you find the case studies and reflections shared by other professionals and parents' useful.

Much like a sunflower, which I chose for the cover of the book, I would like you to consider the start of your journey just as the sunflower does, as a seed. This is your **BEING**: the beginning of your professional journey where you discover your sense of being and reflect upon who you are as an individual and an early year's practitioner.

Following being, I would like you to imagine how a seed is then transported to a pot where it belongs for a short while whilst it germinates. During the germination stage, the seed is nurtured with water and sunlight in the hope it begins to shoot and be strong enough to then be planted outside where it will turn its face to the sun and **THRIVE**.

I have used these themes which I very much hope you can relate to in your journey into Early Years, where you will develop from **BEING** to **BELONGING** and to **THRIVING**.

Each theme is divided into several chapters. As a student, you may wish to begin with the theme of **BEING** and work through the book systematically. Having said that, as you begin to work on your assignments, observations, and reflections, you may interact with different themes and chapters according to your needs. As a tutor or assessor, you may wish to move between themes and chapters to support the delivery of modules.

Each chapter begins with a short introduction and the learning opportunities you will explore. The learning opportunities are represented as 'seeds of knowledge', and each seed is a different topic within the chapter.

At the end of each chapter, you will be invited to reflect upon how you might apply the new seeds of knowledge to your future professional practice and/or studies.

Before you begin to delve into the themes of the book, I feel it is important to share with you my own professional journey of **BEING, BELONGING,** and **THRIVING.**

My **BEING** began at a career's interview where I was advised to go into employment as opposed to college. However, I chose to study at my local Further Education (FE) college and became an NNEB. My first sense of **BELONGING** was as an NNEB in a primary school. For over 20 years, I worked across Nursery, Key stage 1 and 2, before working in a special educational needs setting.

Introduction

My journey towards **THRIVING** began with my foundation degree in Childhood Studies and the many years of studying that followed. Today, I am a qualified lecturer, an external Higher Education (HE) examiner, and an established author, and my thriving continues as I aim to complete my PhD.

It's now time to for you to commence your journey.

Being

BEING is the first theme in this book. As an author and educator, I believe that the concept of **BEING** represents the beginning of your journey as an Early Years practitioner. The beginning of a journey where you will begin to develop your personal and professional values. In the theme of **BEING**, you are laying down the foundations of a career where you will begin to grow and flourish, **BELONG**, and **THRIVE**.

The theme of **BEING** explores the following:

Chapter 1 – The Curious Practitioner

In this chapter, you will have the opportunity to consider how curious you are. You will be able to reflect upon why being curious is important in your role as an Early Years practitioner.

Chapter 2 – The Critically Informed Practitioner

In this chapter, you will explore what is critical thinking and critical analysis. You will have the opportunity to consider how to apply these skills in your role as a critically informed practitioner.

Chapter 3 – The Humanistic Practitioner

In this chapter, you will explore the topics humanism and attachment. You will engage with humanistic and attachment theory and reflect upon how these apply to your role as a humanistic practitioner.

Chapter 4 – The Observant Practitioner

In this chapter, you will be introduced to different observation types and how observation informs assessment and planning. You will also be encouraged to observe the observer.

Belonging

The next theme is **BELONGING.** Having explored the theme of **BEING,** you are now ready to connect theory and practice as you feel a sense of **BELONGING** within your community of practice and your Early Years vocational training and/or setting. Within this theme, you will begin to explore concepts such as play, creativity, inclusion, and within this theme, you will begin to explore concepts such as play, creativity and inclusion. These chapters offer you a starting point for further research in your role as an Early Years practitioner.

The theme of **BELONGING** explores the following:

Chapter 5 – The Playful Practitioner

In this chapter, you will define play. You will also consider the importance of learning how to play yourself alongside the stages and types of play you will encounter in your professional practice. This chapter offers you a snapshot of some of the approaches to play as you begin your Early Years practice. There are many more approaches which you may wish to research further.

Chapter 6 – The Creative Practitioner

In this chapter, you will define creativity and consider the qualities you need to be a creative practitioner. You will explore possibility thinking and the stages of creativity.

Chapter 7 – The Inclusive Practitioner

In this chapter, you will be introduced to the terminology and acronyms that you will encounter as an inclusive practitioner. You will explore your personal values and you will explore your personal values and beliefs and consider how your values align to Early Years settings and the wider society. You will also examine models of disability, legislation, frameworks, policies, and procedures.

 Thriving

In this theme, you will build upon themes of **BEING** and **BELONGING** and apply your skills and knowledge as you **THRIVE** as an Early Years practitioner.

The theme of **THRIVING** includes the following:

Chapter 8 – The Reflective Practitioner

In this chapter, you will begin to explore what is reflection and reflective practice. You will be introduced to the concept of reflective activism and a range of reflective theory, all of which will support you in your academic and professional practice. The chapter ends with an overview of how to write reflectively.

Chapter 9 – The Research Practitioner

In this chapter, you will be introduced to what is research and how research informs you as an early year's practitioner. You will reflect upon the qualities you need as a research practitioner and how you can apply these qualities to your research journey. You will become familiar with key research terminology and be able to use a research design template to help you plan your research.

Chapter 10 – The Developing Practitioner

In this chapter, you will examine the benefits of professional development and ways in which to engage, reflect, and capture your development.

Whilst the contents of the book are set out in the three themes, **BEING, BELONGING** and **THRIVING,** you can use this book in any order that best suits your learning and development.

My hope is that you will be able to visualise your journey using the three key themes, reflect upon the contents of the chapters, and be able to apply all you have learnt to your day-to-day professional practice within Early Years.

Introduction

How to Use This Book

Within the book, you will find three icons which are aligned to several activities, case studies, or reflections.

The icons are roots, shoots, and blooms.

Roots – Reflective Questions

The roots icon will give you the opportunity to stop and reflect. You can spend time answering the reflective questions.

Shoots – Journal Activity

The shoot icon will give you the opportunity to complete a journal activity. You can spent some time reflecting upon your reading, as well journaling your responses to the refelctive questions set within the book. You also have the opportunity to journal and summarise your learning at the end of each chapter, personal, and you can revisit any of the journal activities more than once as part of your professional and reflective journey.

Blooms – Reflective Account

The Sunflower icon invites you to read a reflective account. Each reflective account will give you a different perspective of professional practice. At the end of the reflective account, you will be able to answer a set of reflective questions and contemplate on the key messages from the account.

 Planting Your Seeds of Knowledge and Understanding

At the end of each chapter, you will see a captured image of an Early Years practitioner in action, a play activity, an infographic, as well as a set of questions.

You can use this opportunity to reflect upon the topics you have covered from each chapter and either journal your thoughts or merely sit a while and reflect.

Being

Be prepared to be perfectly imperfect, be prepared for wins and challenges, but most of all be prepared to be YOU.

Annie Pendrey

DOI: 10.4324/9781003361442-1

The Curious Practitioner

Welcome to the first chapter of this book, The Curious Practitioner. The mere fact that you have picked up this book shows you are curious to learn, develop, and thrive as an Early Years practitioner. This chapter explores the concept of curiosity and how being curious will support you at the start and throughout your academic and professional journey in Early Years.

This chapter invites you to reflect upon your childhood memories of curiosity. There is also the opportunity to journal and reflect upon narratives shared by other Early Years professionals before reflecting upon why you need to be a curious practitioner.

The seeds of knowledge explored within the chapter are:

Curiosity
Epistemic curiosity
Curious practitioners: Your academic practice
Curious Practitioners: Your professional practice
The ladder of participation and curiosity

DOI: 10.4324/9781003361442-2

Curiosity

Journal Activity – Capturing Curiosity

Let's begin this chapter with your reflective journal. Take some time to reflect and answer the following questions. Journal your responses.

Can you think of a time in your childhood when you were curious?

What were you doing?

What did you discover?

Why do you feel it was a curious experience?

What is curiosity?

Let me share with you my first childhood memory of curiosity and why I feel it is important to reflect upon our first memories of childhood before we can begin to define curiosity.

My first childhood memory of being curious is a memory of exploration, experimentation, and play. I was about five years old and playing alone in my back garden. I recall my garden being surrounded with hedges and always filled with birds. My dad used to sit with me and tell me the name of each bird, and I recall him making me a bird bath in the garden out of some bits and bobs. The bath even had a pretend tap so I could pretend to turn the tap on so the bath could be filled with fresh water for the birds.

One day whilst out in the garden, I recall watching one bird flying in and out of one of the hedges several times. I recall being fascinated as to why they were so busy. So, whilst this little bird flew out of the hedge, I decided to force my head into the hedge. I could not see anything straight away and so I began to push myself deeper into the hedge, forcing in my head, hair, and shoulders. It was then I could hear the cheeping of baby birds at the same time as my mom calling me in for dinner. Of course, by this point, my hair was tangling in the hedge, and I was quite stuck!

I could not free myself. I recall shouting, 'Mom, help!' My Mom arrived, and I clearly remember her not shouting at me for being stuck headfirst in the hedge. Instead, she freed me from the hedge and went on to explain how I should not have been disturbing the baby birds. However, she did not scold me for being curious.

Curiosity in children and adults should be celebrated and nurtured. As Early Years practitioners, we should be curious and not afraid to explore, experiment, and apply our curiosity to our academic and professional practice. Daniel Berlyne (1960) defines curiosity as an inner drive. I understand this to be the internal drive we have as Early Years practitioners to be curious about our professional practice, to ask questions, and to seek out new ideas and concepts. Your studies and your work environment should stir and not crush your curiosity. As adults, we should possibly be more of our two-year-old selves, the-two-year-old who constantly asks, 'why?' The two-year-old who is inquisitive and questions the question.

Berlyne's (1960) work introduced me to the term epistemic curiosity. Would it be a pun, if I were to say that the very term made me curious? If so, I do not apologise, as it is important to be curious about new words, concepts, and ideas and to then go and explore even further and apply any new knowledge to your role as an Early Years practitioner.

Being

Epistemic Curiosity

Epistemic curiosity is your inner drive, your desire to fill gaps in your knowledge. Epistemic curiosity is the motivation to learn new ideas, concepts, approaches, and theory. You have already displayed your epistemic curiosity and desire to learn new things by interacting with this book. It is now time to put your epistemic curiosity to good use and apply it to your academic and professional practice.

Now you have begun to think about curiosity, now is a good opportunity to stop and reflect. What do you feel you need to be more curious about? And how can you show your tutors and vocational setting colleagues you are a curious practitioner?

 **Reflective Questions**

What are you curious about?

How can you fill the gaps in your knowledge?

What support do you need?

Why do you feel you need to be a curious practitioner?

Now you have taken time to reflect about curiosity, take time to read some reflective accounts from practitioners about curiosity.

Consider how each of the reflective accounts define curiosity.

Reflective Account

Fozia is an Early Years Lecturer and shares her thoughts on curiosity.

Read her account and then pause, contemplate, and reflect.

Take time to answer the reflective questions.

There is a saying, 'curiosity killed the cat' but luckily, being curious doesn't kill you. Being curious means, being willing to open our minds to new ideas, new concepts, and a willingness to be critical of our surroundings and embrace what was once unknown. By being curious we can challenge our experiences and change how we practice. To be truly curious, we cannot take things for what they are, we must question further and explore for a deeper insight, and we must think outside of the box. For example, we can look at an object and think of what its general, intended uses are, but to be curious we would think of all the possibilities of how this one object can be used in different ways.

By doing this we are broadening our minds and how we perceive things. Curiosity means to unravel all the entanglements in our minds, to find answers for the smallest of questions that we think of, and to go forth and feed that little spark in our minds that tells us to push forward to see what we can lead to. From this curiosity, we see that the opportunities are actually endless depending on just how curious you want to be or how curious you can be, or even how curious we have learnt to be.

Fostering curiosity in Early Years allows young children to utilise their newfound thinking skills. Allowing children to be free thinkers, to allow them to question their surroundings and solve problems, will build on their curiosity. In some ways, curiosity can be seen as a skill of the mind that can be developed in children but needs the time, effort, and support of practitioners. To allow children to flourish, and develop curiosity, practitioners would need to create spaces and environments that allow children to explore outside of the norm of the current framework.

Being curious, from an educational point of view, will allow the individual to gain further knowledge. The same concept of thinking outside of the box allows you to think more widely which equates to gaining more knowledge. Questioning topics, or areas of learning, will again broaden knowledge; it is that 'not taking things for what they are' mindset which makes an individual question and be curious, resulting in more knowledge and understanding.

It is important for children to have this mindset in order to grow up and become thinkers, problem solvers, utilising their minds to their full potential.

Future practitioners need to be curious, as we are role models to the young children we work with.

If we show children that as practitioners we question, we are problem solvers, we are creative, and we are curious, it is more likely that some of this will rub off onto children and students whom we work with. If we plan and implement activities and sessions that encourage children and students to be curious from a young age, it is more likely that this will become a habit, it will become a skill that they gain and use for their futures.

Reflective Questions

What is the key message Fozia is trying to say in her reflective account?

Do you agree with her reflections, if so, why?

Why is it important for us as practitioners to be curious?

How will being curious impact upon the young children you work with?

Reflective Account

Lisa is the Nursery Manager and SENCO at Playdays Nursery.

Lisa and the team of practitioners share with you their reflections about curiosity.

Curiosity...where to start!

As Early Years practitioners, we strive to create wonder and joy in our environment and planning. We spend time creating, planning, and carefully constructing play experiences and spaces, and we do all of this to inspire and to evoke children's curiosity. All these reasons are valid and are intrinsic to all we do as active practitioners, but I often wonder do we really step back and think about curiosity?

What is it that makes us curious as humans, are some of us more curious than others, and why? When we plan and create with a vision in mind of an expected response from children, is it always the response we wanted? Often I suspect it isn't.

As an Early Years Manager, I began to reflect further. I decided I wanted to explore my teams' thinking around their perspectives of children's curiosity within our setting. I felt a good place to start would be to unpick the term curiosity; in other words, what makes us curious?

We began to explore this question by taking some time to reflect on what it meant. That question alone seemed challenging ... where to begin! So instead of tackling such a complex question, we chatted about a simpler way to try to explore our own thoughts around curiosity. After much coffee, biscuits, and chats, we decided to create a curiosity board in the staff room area. The team chose an image and anonymously wrote a statement about why this image evoked curiosity for them personally. The images were shared in the reflective space, and some images had similar themes but with very different personal perspectives.

We spent time looking at the images and reading the reflections; they were all so unique and offered such diverse perspectives around our own curiosity. This was a truly fascinating experience for us all; the images and perspectives were anonymous, yet there was a familiarity about the written perspectives. Our small team began to recognise who was behind the images and words. We assumed this was because of our small team and setting; however, after further reflection, we realised there were other factors involved.

As a team, we listen to each other, and we value each other's voices, attributes, and personality.

You may ask yourself why and how this could be linked to supporting experiences and curiosity for our little ones; our response would be they are the same as we are as adults, individual with differing perspectives. The experiences we assume would evoke curiosity may not; the carefully beautifully planned play experience may not be a triumph for all ... but that's ok!

As a team, we felt the key to really understanding children's curiosity is to carefully and gently watch, listen, and recognise who they are as individuals. This is no different to how we explored curiosity as a team; we recognise each other's perspectives, and we listen, value, and gently encourage.

Upon reflection, for me, curiosity, joy, awe, and wonder can always be found in experiences if we just take time to step back, pause, and truly tune in to what we are seeing and hearing. Maybe if we relax a little and trust in the fact that we know our little ones, we may be able to recognise natural curiosity in simple experiences.

We intend to continue to develop our own curiosity in the same way that we encourage curiosity in our children. As practitioners, it may be helpful to stop and pause and reflect together through simple activities to explore our own curiosity. It doesn't have to be complicated or expensive, just take time to tune in to each other as well as our little ones.

FIGURE 1.1   Playdays Nursery Curiosity Board

Reflective Questions

What do you feel are some of the key messages from Lisa's reflective account?

How can you embed some of the ideas of this reflective account to your professional practice?

What and why is it important to work with others to capture children's curiosity as well as your own?

Curious Practitioners

In this part of the chapter, you will explore why we need to be curious as practitioners and how curiosity can inform your academic and professional practice.

Appreciating and reflecting upon our own levels of curiosity as practitioners are essential before we can then begin to nurture children's curiosity.

So, how do you ensure you remain curious and how do you apply curiosity to your studies and your professional practice?

For me, I think this is about questioning, questioning the question, and maybe being a little more egocentric and asking why? Asking yourself why, questioning your colleagues, your peers, and your tutors in a non-argumentative way, asking them why? This is the start of not only being a curious practitioner but also a reflective practitioner. (Reflection and The Reflective Practitioner are covered in Chapter 8). You need to almost return to your two-year-old self, two-year old's love to ask why and they do so repeatedly.

Curious Practitioners: Your Academic Practice

Being curious in your academic studies will support you to examine literature and develop your critical thinking skills, which will then support you to critically analyse and critically reflect in your written work. Being curious, and being a critical thinker, and reflector will support you as you begin to complete essays, reports, and reflective accounts. Moreover, these skills will also benefit you in your vocational practice as you gain the confidence to question the theoretical frameworks, legislation, policies, and curriculums that are in place in the Early Years and Education sector.

You will read more about critical thinking and being theoretically informed in Chapter 2, but for now, I wish to share with you a concept I share with all my students when they begin their academic journey. It is something you can adopt and use throughout your studies and career and that is to 'Think like a dragon'.

I usually begin a new session of teaching with considering what is thinking? What does it mean to you? I also invite students to tell me if they think they are philosophers. At this point, I usually define what philosophy means. Philosophy in its broadest meaning is to use your mind to inquire, to think, and to question. So, for example, to not merely accept all I might say in a lesson but to question my knowledge, to question the information that is presented to you and to seek meaning and understanding.

So, how is this related to thinking like a dragon? Let me explain. When new information is presented to you, take time to read and interpret the information. But then maybe breathe a little fire over the words, as a dragon would! This is the start of you pulling apart the information, thinking more about what has been presented to you and being curious. Continue being more dragon, spread your wings and research, continuously seek new information. You should even flap your wings a little and by this I mean, don't just accept the literature you may have read, flap your wings, make some noise, and agree or disagree, applying your critical thinking skills. This is all part of being a curious practitioner and thinking like a dragon!

 Reflective Questions

Do you currently feel you are a curious practitioner? If not, why not?

How can you improve this?

Think about a previous piece of reading, were you curious enough about its content?

How will being more curious in your studies support your academic journey?

How can you be more curious in your professional practice?

Take time to think if you need any support from your tutors or mentor at this point in your academic journey. What do you need and how can you receive this support?

Curious Practitioners: Your Professional Practice

Let's begin this part of your curious journey with a journal activity.

Journal Activity – Curious Practitioners and Your Professional Practice

Open a page of your journal and use the heading Curious Practitioners and Your Professional Practice.

Now think about a recent activity you have undertaken or observed with children.

Next, read the following questions, reflect, and scribe your responses.

You can share these answers with your peers, mentor, or tutor. Or keep your reflections to yourself but maybe revisit them as you progress on your professional and academic journey.

Reflect and answer:

What was the aim of the activity?

Was it child led, adult led, or both?

Do you feel the children and/or the practitioner was curious? How?

What do you feel you would have changed to improve the activity?

Challenge – do you feel as a practitioner we are driven by the curriculum? Does this hinder our curiosity?

You may not have all the answers to these questions. You might wish to reflect upon these at different points in your learning. You just need to be continuously curious about your professional practice. Being curious will benefit the children and the families with whom you work.

Maybe after you have attempted this journal activity, you could revisit it once you have read about Harts ladder of participation. Hart's ladder of participation will lead you to reflect upon your professional practice, asking you to reflect upon your professional practice. For example, you might wish to reflect upon how the learning opportunities you provide ensure every child can be curious.

Hart's Ladder of Participation

Hart's (2013) model has eight rungs and two main zones, which Hart calls 'Non-Participation' and 'Degrees of Participation'. The top five rungs, in the 'Participation' zone, all represent different but valid forms of participation whilst the three lowest rungs are all designated as 'non-participation'.

Hart's ladder of participation has eight rungs and is a model that encourages you to reflect and to be curious when you are planning and designing activities or sessions for children. It is just one approach that will make you think about the purpose of the activity/session, how much the child/ren are involved, and their level of curiosity and learning. It will encourage you to critically reflect upon whether what you are designing is product driven and too adult led as opposed to child initiated and process driven.

Let's journal Hart's Ladder of Participation. This will help you to further understand and apply Hart's thinking.

 **Journal Activity – Hart's Ladder of Participation**

Take some time to draw a ladder and label the ladder rungs from 1 to 8.

Start from the bottom rung of the ladder, number 1, and label **manipulation,** and then work up the ladder, labelling each rung as follows:

1. **Manipulation**
2. **Decoration**
3. **Tokenism**
4. **Assigned and informed**
5. **Consulted and informed**
6. **Adult initiated, shared decisions with the child**
7. **Child initiated and directed**
8. **Child initiated, shared decisions with adults**

FIGURE 1.2   An outline of a ladder

Once you have done this, read the following explanations of each rung of the ladder and rewrite each explanation in your own words. This will help your understanding of Hart's Ladder of participation and help you reflect and apply this theory to your professional practice. Don't forget to apply your critical thinking and critical analysis.

Hart suggests that the top five rings of the ladder are in what he called the participation zone, where the child has valid interactions with experience and is a participant, whereas the lower three rungs of the ladder are labelled as non-participation.

Each rung is then broken down into the eight rungs. These are:

1. **Manipulation**
   The first rung of the ladder is where there is little child participation. The child is directed during adult-led activities.
2. **Decoration**
   This is where the child may understand the purpose of the activity/experience, but the activity is still adult-led, and the child has had no input in how this activity was planned.

3. **Tokenism**

   In this rung of the ladder, the activity is still adult led, but the child may be consulted somewhat. However, this consultation is limited, and the child receives little opportunity to give the adult feedback on the activity and to be heard.

4. **Assigned and informed**

   The fourth rung of the ladder is where a child has a role within the adult-led activity. The child has more involvement in the decision making process of the activity.

5. **Consulted and informed**

   In this rung of the ladder, the adult-led activity does include the child. The child is consulted and informed about the activity, and the child's input is considered by the adult.

6. **Adult initiated, shared decisions with the child**

   The sixth rung of the ladder is where the adult-led activity involves joint decision making between the child and the adult.

7. **Child initiated and directed**

   Towards the top of the ladder, the child is now leading their own activities with little input from the adult.

8. **Child initiated, shared decisions with adults**

   The final rung of the ladder is where Hart believes that there is a real partnership between adult and child. Both parties share decision making in the child-led activity.

The aim of exploring Hart's ladder of participation is for you to be curious and reflective about your professional practice. It is also a reminder for you to remain curious throughout your professional career and to continuously reflect upon your pedagogical approaches.

Being

Having explored Hart's ladder of participation, you need to remind yourself of the importance of remaining curious: to take risks in your pedagogical approaches with young children and reflect upon how our education system should spark joy, awe, and wonder for our young children.

Remaining curious is also about how as a practitioner you remain focused on the process of learning and not always the product. By this I mean, ensuring you do not fall into the trap of producing batches of celebration cards, products that are adult led, and activities which squash children's curiosity. You need to continuously reflect upon how children are engaged in their learning and ask yourself the following reflective questions.

Reflective Questions

Is the activity and/or the environment sparking curiosity?

Am I enabling the child/children to be curious?

Is the activity child led? If I were to reimagine this activity as a young child, what would I want to do? Would it spark my curiosity?

What levels of participation are there for the child/children?

Once you have reflected upon these questions, you might wish to read the reflective practitioner (Chapter 8) and consider how your answers inform your reflective activism.

Planting your seeds of knowledge and understanding

At the end of this chapter, you are now ready to plant the seeds of knowledge you have discovered about curiosity. You are now ready to reflect upon your understanding of how you will be a curious practitioner in your professional practice.

Take a moment to look back at the topics, and using the image, reflect upon:

What is curiosity?

Why do we need to be curious practitioners?

How can we support children's curiosity?

Take time to think about when you next go into your setting, how will you promote curiosity?

Curiosity

C – **Curiosity** should be an

U – **Unbelievable** experience where you don't mind a little

R – **Risk Taking**. Curiosity is when you are

I – **Inquisitive** and

O – **Open** to new and

U – **Unexpected** experiences and always

S – **Seeking** a challenge!

Be a **CURIOUS** Practitioner.

Annie Pendrey

FIGURE 1.3 Children's hands on a light box

2 The Critically Informed Practitioner

In this chapter, you will be encouraged to reflect about how you are informed as a practitioner. What types of sources are available to you that informs your professional practice? You will also be introduced to what is critical thinking and critical analysis and how to apply these skills when you are accessing different types of information.

The seeds of knowledge explored within the chapter are as follows:

Critical thinking
Critical analysis
Bias
Informed practitioners
Critically informed practitioners

Critical Thinking

As practitioners, we often think on our feet, what we might call in-the-moment thinking. However, we also need to apply critical

DOI: 10.4324/9781003361442-3

thinking to our professional practice. You will also apply critical thinking to your academic studies.

Let's begin with the concept of thinking! How many thoughts do you have each day? I cannot begin to imagine an answer. We are bombarded each day with directions, commands, and messages. As an early year's practitioner, you will need to use your thinking skills to develop your knowledge of children's learning and development. You will need to use your thinking skills to seek out different perspectives within literature, apply reasoning, defend your viewpoint and find solutions to issues when supporting children, young people and families.

And so, you need to consider and explore what is critical thinking and how you can become more of a critical thinker?

Critical thinking supports you to uncover the truth from the information. Critical thinking is about being non-bias and non-judgemental. It is about identifying issues, gathering the truth to make well-informed decisions based on evidence, and having the ability to substantiate your argument.

Words, knowledge, and theory are important to a critical thinker. Critical thinkers use words, knowledge, and theory to reflect, to analyse, and to be an advocate and reflective activist.

Critical Analysis

In addition to critical thinking, you also need to apply critical analysis to your academic studies and professional practice.

Critical analysis is a process of evaluating information, arguments, or evidence to form a well-supported and informed judgment or conclusion. These judgements and conclusions will inform your professional practice. Critical analysis involves carefully examining a piece of information, considering its strengths and weaknesses, and making an objective assessment. This can involve analysing data, ideas, or arguments in a systematic and structured manner using critical thinking skills to assess their validity and reliability. In simple terms, this means that when you are presented with a piece of information, you should always apply a critical lens and consider the information from different perspectives. This is critical analysis.

Critical analysis requires an objective and analytical mind-set as well as an ability to understand and assess complex information. It requires the development of critical thinking skills, such as the ability to identify and evaluate arguments, recognise biases and assumptions, and draw well-supported conclusions. As a critically informed practitioner, you should apply these skills to a range of information. The aim being that you identify, evaluate, and analyse the key information to form a well-considered conclusion.

Overall, critical analysis is a valuable tool for all practitioners. It is a tool which will support you to make informed decisions based on evidence. In simple terms, this means that when you are presented with a piece of information, you should always apply a critical lens and consider the information from different perspectives. This is critical analysis.

Bias

The topic of bias is multi-faceted. For this chapter, you will briefly explore what bias is and how it relates to being a critically informed practitioner. Bias can be defined as a prejudice, a feeling, an inclination, and/or distortion of a person or a group.

As a critically informed practitioner, you need to be honest and open about your personal bias when interacting with information. For example, when you read an article, you need to be aware of your personal bias as this may influence how you interpret the information.

You need to be reflective and consider other's perspectives even if their perspectives conflict with your personal beliefs and values. It is important to view information, for example, when reading an article, as you read it, be aware of your bias so that you can make informed decision. You need to continuously seek what is knowledge and what is truth. This involves reflecting upon how history and/or your own values and beliefs shape our views and self-lens.

Being

Informed Practitioners

Having explored critical thinking and critical analysis, you now need to be aware of why it is important to use these skills in order to be a critically informed practitioner.

Let's begin with a journal activity exploring how we are informed as early years practitioners.

Journal Activity – Informed Practitioners

Open a page of your journal and mind map, how many ways you are informed? How many ways are pieces of information shared with you and how do you feel these inform your professional practice?

Let me give you an example, we are all informed by media. Now think about the wealth of information that is available on social media and how this information informs you as an early years practitioner?

Challenge yourself and consider is all the information informative, if not, why not?

As you travel through this book, you will be introduced to several sources of information that you will interact with as part of your professional journey. You can revisit the journal activity and add further detail to your initial thoughts. The key message is that it is vitally important that as critically informed practitioners, we listen to our children, young people, and families.

In addition to our listening skills are our critical thinking and critical analysis skills. As practitioners, we need to draw upon research, innovations, more experienced practitioners, and history to discover, reflect, and critique new information. By doing this, we are showing how we can adapt and change and how we must appreciate other perspectives. By doing so, this will inform our professional practice.

So, how are we informed as early years practitioners? There are several ways, these include the following:

Informed by Parents/Carers, Children, and Young People

These are our richest assets in early years and education. They are the service users, and as practitioners, we need to find as many ways as possible to listen to their voices. You may hear the term parents/carers as partners or parents/carers as first educators. Both terms are important as it makes us reflect upon how we need to build relationships with our parents/carers so that they can openly inform us of their child's wishes, needs, likes, and dislikes.

We must collaborate with our parents/carers so that the information sharing is continuous and supports our professional practice. Parents/carers have information regarding their child's culture, medical needs, learning preferences, and so much more. We need all this information so that we can fully support their child. A parent/carer is very much their child's advocate.

Children also inform us. Children's perspectives and lived experiences inform our professional practice. How we capture these and their voices is achieved by communicating verbally and non-verbally with your children, discovering forms of communication which suit each child so that they can inform you of their likes, needs, interests, thoughts, and opinions.

We must also utilise our observation skills and take information from our observations of the child to inform our professional practice, to inform our planning, and to communicate the information sourced to the child's parents/carers. It is also important to gain a different perspective of the child, and this may be done by reading others practitioners observations whose reflective lens may have captured something you may not have. This will give you a more in-depth view critical analysis of the child. (Refer to both Chapters 4 and 8 for more information about observation and reflection.)

Informed by Professionals

You will work with and alongside many professionals in your early year's career. Each professional has a unique academic background and experience which will inform your practice.

For example, you may work with any of the following:

- Teachers
- Health visitors, doctors, and other medical staff
- Youth workers
- Social workers
- Educational psychologists
- Counsellors
- Speech and language therapists
- SENCOs
- Housing services
- Police
- Other voluntary organisations and charities

Professionals inform you through communication, directly or indirectly. You may also be informed by other professionals through training courses or in meetings which concern a child in your care.

Take time to network with other professionals and gain a different perspective of education and early years.

Use their guidance and expertise to inform your professional practice. It may also be that some of these professionals have publications and research you can interact with as an additional source of information.

So, share your critical perspective, thinking, and thoughts with others. Listen to other professionals, take time to critically think and analyse other perspectives, but don't be afraid to share your own perspective. As professionals, we all have the best interests of the child at heart, and we all have a unique set of skills and knowledge in our role as a young child's advocate.

Informed by Research

There is a wealth of research available to you as practitioners. Research findings are presented in journal articles, in publications, at conferences, and across social media. Whilst you engage in research, you should always apply your critical lens. As you engage with research, seek out any bias, question the validity and reliability of the research. Reflect and consider if the research is trustworthy. Will it inform your professional practice?. It is also good practice to check the date of the research, the country in which the research took place, and the number of participants in the research. These are all factors to consider in any research you read and wish to apply to your academic studies or professional practice. This involves you scrutinising and applying your critical skills.

For example, if you read a magazine article, this may be only the author's opinion, whereas an academic journal is usually peer-reviewed; this means they are subjected to other's critical lens and so may offer you a more substantiated and objective viewpoint.

 ## Journal Activity – Beginning to Critique

A good starting point is to first read the article/journal and using your journal begin to write down the key points and messages you have taken from the reading.

Is the research current, valid, objective, and trustworthy?

Do you agree with all the points raised?

> What do you disagree with and why?
>
> Has this research helped you become critically and theoretically informed?
>
> What do you feel you need to research further following reading this piece of research?

Informed by Theory

What is a theory? A theory is a well-substantiated explanation of an aspect of our world. For you as a practitioner, this is the world of education and early years. A theory is usually based on a body of evidence. The theory can then be used to support you in understanding a child's development, learning, and/or behaviour for example. You can apply theory to your observations of children and young people.

You will explore a range of theory and theorists, such as theories of learning and development, reflective theories, theories about leadership, care, and many more topics. All theories provide you with a framework which you can use to help you understand and appreciate a child's reaction or a child's stage of development for example.

However, don't be fearful of having an enquiring mind. Question and critically analyse each theory. This level of critical thinking and analysis shows you are a critically informed practitioner.

Informed by Pioneers

You will also be informed by pioneers. A pioneer is someone who has explored, developed, and applied their concepts to their professional practice and gone on to share their ideas and approaches with others. For example, there are several pioneers of play. These pioneers have researched and developed aspects of play. Their mission is to inspire you to reflect and apply their work to your practice.

There are many pioneers in early years and education, and you will be introduced to these as part of your academic and/or professional learning and development. In this chapter, you are not being introduced to the vast number of pioneers but encouraged to reflect how each pioneer may influence your professional practice in the future.

Informed by Media

In the world we live, it is almost impossible not to be informed by media. Media presents itself to us as newspapers, television, radio, online news websites, and social media platforms. The media reports on current events both locally and internationally.

Social media platforms such as X, Facebook, and Instagram are also becoming important sources of news. Users can follow news organisations and journalists to receive breaking news alerts and updates. You can join groups that discuss current topics surrounding early years and education. However, it is important to verify the credibility of each source and every group you might join.

As a critically informed practitioner, you need to view all sources critically. You need to remove all bias from the sources as they may influence how you interpret the information.

Informed by Innovation

The world of education is ever-changing and with this comes innovation. Innovation includes new forms of technology, changes in curriculum, pedagogical approaches, and much more.

Artificial Intelligence, for example, is now part of our world and an innovation that will possibly impact upon how you plan or produce documents. However, with any innovation in the field of education, you should remain curious and critically informed. Innovations can provide you with a fresh approach and a new way of thinking; update your skills and knowledge but continue to be critical and make informed decisions as to their application to your professional practice.

Being

Critically Informed Practitioner

To conclude, a critically informed practitioner is you! You are the practitioner who has developed an awareness of how different information can inform your professional practice. However, you have a deeper understanding now of how not to merely accept all sources of information but to apply your critical thinking skills when interacting with the information.

So, as you move forward in your journey of being, belonging to thriving, continue to commit to ongoing reflection, critical thinking, and critical analysis in ensuring all children's needs, wishes, and rights are met.

Planting your seeds of knowledge and understanding

At the end of this chapter, you are now ready to plant the seeds of knowledge you have discovered about critical thinking, critical analysis, and how you are informed as a practitioner.

You are now ready to reflect upon your understanding of how you will be a critically informed practitioner in your professional practice.

Take a moment to look back at the topics, and using the image, reflect upon:

What is critical thinking and critical analysis?

Why do we need to apply these skills in our professional capacity?

How do these skills support our children, young people, and parents?

The practitioner in the image (Figure 2.1) is using an image of children playing to critically analyse the child's learning and development. The use of images is a powerful tool for applying your critical thinking and critical analysis.

FIGURE 2.1 Practitioners critically thinking and reflecting

3 | The Humanistic Practitioner

In this chapter, you will explore the term humanism and consider how this term relates to a you as a humanistic practitioner. You will be introduced to some of the different forms of attachments and the part you play as a humanistic practitioner in developing an attachment and professional relationships with children.

The seeds of knowledge explored within the chapter are as follows:

Humanism
Humanistic theory
Attachment and attachment theory
Professional love and relationships

Humanism

As Early Years practitioners, whenever you interact with young children, you do this from a nurturing and humanistic stance. As you begin to capture your observations and reflective accounts,

DOI: 10.4324/9781003361442-4

you will begin to recognise how invaluable these humanistic interactions are in supporting children's well-being and development.

So, what is humanism? Humanism is simply defined as the innate human potential to 'do good'. Humanism focuses on human beings being free to act and control their own intentions. It focuses on human values, interests, abilities, needs, worth, and dignity.

As you care and nurture each child in your care, you will soon begin to recognise this as humanistic practice. This humanistic practice is significant from the very beginning of a child's learning, and it is vital that it continues throughout their journey.

The journey a child takes with you needs some essential components such as food, warmth, security, comfort, and companionship. All these components support a child's being, belonging, and thriving. Ensuring you supply these components is part of your humaisitic approach. You are in a priviledged position to support all the children in your care, watching them devlop and thrive.

Humanistic Theory

Humanism has a range of theorists you can explore and apply to your professional practice. In this chapter, you will explore the work of Maslow and Rogers. The overview of each theory will support you to understand the concept of each theory and then apply this theory to your everyday practice. You can then apply your critical and reflective lens to consider how humanistic theory impacts upon the young children and families with whom you work.

The work of Maslow and Rogers seeks to encourage you to reflect upon how each theory impacts upon your work as a humanistic practitioner. Of course, as with all theory, do not be afraid to apply your critical thinking and critical analysis considering the pros and cons of each theory.

Read Maslow and Rogers's theory and take time to use the summary to add reflective notes to your reflective journal.

Being

Abraham Maslow (1943)

Overview of Theory

Abraham Maslow's (1943) theory is simply represented as a triangle. Maslow leads us to believe that every human needs their basic needs met before they can self-actualise. Maslow believes that a child needs to have their physiological needs met, then safety, love, and belonging so that the child has a positive self-esteem. Once a child has all these needs met, they will then self-actualise.

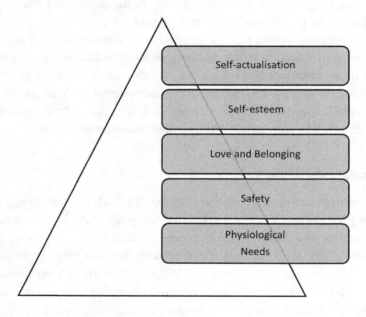

FIGURE 3.1   Maslow's hierarchy of needs

To further explain Maslow's hierarchy of needs, let's explore each layer of the hierarchy and define what this means and how you might apply this to your professional practice as a humanistic practitioner.

Physiological needs are the basic needs we all need to survive such as air, water, warmth, food, shelter, reproduction, and sleep. In your professional practice, reflect upon how a child who may be hungry when they arrive to setting may not feel energised to engage in activities. How could you support this child?

Safety needs include personal resources, security, employment, health, and property. In your professional practice, reflect upon how a child who may not be feeling well from a short- or long-term illness and how this may impact upon the child?

Love and belonging needs include having a sense of connection, friendships, and family. In your professional practice, reflect upon the importance of offering a child a sense of connection and belonging. How do you feel a child without a sense of belonging may feel and what possible impacts might this have upon the child?

Self-esteem needs include strength, freedom, recognition, respect, and self-esteem. In your professional practice, reflect upon how you ensure each child is encouraged and supported to build their self-esteem. You can also begin to consider the possible effects of low self-esteem upon a child.

At the top of Maslow's hierarchy of needs is self-actualisation and in simple terms, this is when as a child or adult you are happy in what you are doing: your achievements. It is when a child or adult feels they have reached their inner potential: they have self-actualised. This is the area of personal growth and discovery and is present throughout one's life.

The work of Maslow and Rogers seeks to encourage you to reflect upon how each theory impacts upon your work as a humanistic practitioner. Of course, as with all theory, do not be afraid to apply your critical thinking and critical analysis considering the pros and cons of each theory.

Read Maslow and Rogers's theory and take time to use the summary to add reflective notes to your reflective journal.

Applying Theory to Professional Practice

Maslow's hierarchy of needs may be helpful as you are developing your relationships in your setting, whether you are already in practice or beginning your journey as a student. It offers you a visual reminder of your role as humanistic practitioner role and how you can ensure children receive their basic needs and go on to self-actualise.

You need to work and communicate with other professionals and explore how you can ensure all the child's needs are met. Forming relationships with other professionals and parents is key as a humanistic practitioner in working as a partnership to support your children and families. It may be that the support the child/ren and families need is outside agencies.

Summarise This Theory in Your Reflective Journal and Apply to Your Professional Practice

Summarise Maslow's theory in your reflective journal.

Create an imaginary child, reflect upon their needs, and apply Maslow's theory to your professional practice. How will you support the child to self-actualise?

Now, challenge yourself and apply your critical thinking and analysis. Can you critique Maslow's theory?

Carl Rogers (1969)

Overview of Theory

Roger's (1969) theory is also humanistic. Rogers's theory has two key terms that you can apply to your role as a humanistic practitioner. These include the following. One term is 'fully functioning person'. A fully functioning person according to Rogers encompasses the whole person and recognises a person's health and well-being. As a humanistic practitioner, you can consider how you ensure you support a child's health and well-being as part of their holistic development.

Another key term of Roger's theory is 'unconditional positive regard'. For you as a humanistic practitioner, this means that you accept very child. You accept every child without judgement and show them unconditional positive regard. This links to that sense of professional love we have as practitioners for our children. This is the genuine respect and empathy we display to our children in our care all of the time.

Applying Theory to Professional Practice

As a humanistic practitioner, Roger's theory suggests that there are certain qualities a fully functioning person demonstrates. For you, you can consider what these are and how you can support these in a young child who is developing a sense of who they are as an individual. Let's explore the qualities Rogers suggests that a fully functioning person possesses but then relate this to a child and more importantly how you can support a child develop these qualities.

Open to New Experiences

As a humanistic practitioner, consider how you encourage all children to be open to new experiences. Consider the ways in which you support them to appreciate and regulate their feelings when attempting new experiences.

Living in the Present

As a humanistic practitioner, you will be supporting children to appreciate the 'here-and-the-now' moments.

Being

Trust

This is a quality you will support in children continuously. You will motivate and encourage each child to trust in themselves and to trust the decisions or risks they take in their learning journey.

Freedom of Choice

As a humanistic practitioner, you will support children to begin to understand how to take responsibility for their own actions but how they also have a sense of freedom. They have a choice in their learning and their play. They also then begin to develop a sense of responsibility for their own actions as they develop and thrive.

Creativity

As a creative practitioner, a playful practitioner, and a humanistic practitioner, you can apply all your skills and knowledge to provide opportunities for creativity. Creativity provides children with a vehicle of learning, an opportunity for expression, and supports children in many aspects of their learning, development, and well-being.

Reliability and Constructiveness

Rogers believes this to be how you as a humanistic practitioner are reliable and responsive to a child's needs. Being reliable will ensure that children feel secure and safe and that as a practitioner you will respond to their needs.

A Rich Full Life

If you consider what it means personally to live a rich full life, you might consider this to be a life that is joyous, happy, and fun. However, Rogers acknowledges that a rich full life is one that does not only have these elements but also involves challenges which bring about pain and despair and goes on to any that fear and courage are also part of a rich full life.

As humanistic practitioner, you need to consider how you support your young children to obtain a rich full life and what you and others can do to ensure that each child can thrive and become a fully functioning child. Your collaboration with other professionals and services is key. Moreover, providing a culture of care, a culture where every child is treated with positive self-regard is key in your role as humanistic practitioner.

Summarise This Theory in Your Reflective Journal and Apply to Your Professional Practice

Summarise Roger's theory.

How do you feel you apply Roger's theory to your professional practice? Give examples.

Can you critique Roger's theory? What do you think are some of the challenges in applying Roger's theory?

Do you promote a culture of care? How? Give examples.

Attachment and Attachment Theory

In this section, you will explore what is meant by attachment and how this links to the professional relationships you form with children and their families and carers.

An attachment is the emotional, lasting connection between two people, the emotional connection and bond you form with the young children in your care.

Children will form attachments and relationships throughout their childhood. These attachments include the following:

Being

Primary Attachments

A primary attachment is the attachment the child makes with their primary caregiver, the person who continuously responds to their needs. In the case of a young baby, this primary attachment is the bond formed between the child and the person who responds to their cries for food, warmth, love, and attention.

Significant Attachments

These attachments are the collection of wider individuals, siblings, grandparents, and the child's key person.

However, you must also consider how some children will have different experiences of attachments and many factors may impact upon the attachments children form with their primary and significant attachments.

As a humanistic practitioner, you will form an attachment and a bond with each child in your care. This is the foundation of an ongoing professional relationship. There are several attachment theories you can relate to your professional practice, but a good point of reference is the work of Bowlby. Bowlby's theory will provide you an overview of how secure attachments are considered significant in supporting a child's healthy development.

Read Bowlby's theory and take time to summarise and reflect how you might apply Bowlby's theory to your professional practice.

John Bowlby (1969) and Mary Ainsworth (1978)

Overview of Theory

John Bowlby's theory focuses on how children form an attachment and emotional bond with their primary caregiver. Bowlby believed this primary caregiver to be the mother and that the critical time of the first two years of a child's life was the most sensitive period for forming attachments. He goes on to say that if attachments are disrupted during this time, it can influence the child's ability to form relationships and other areas of their development. In early years, the primary caregiver is you. You are the person who is available to respond to the needs of the young child. Your responses reassure the child that this adult is available and dependable. According to Bowlby, the child will then begin to understand that their primary caregiver can be trusted and can provide a secure base from which they then go and explore their environment and world.

Bowlby's work on primary attachments and separation anxiety, which you may wish to research further, particularly influenced Mary Ainsworth who developed his theory further. Ainsworth's stranger situation experiment, and her observations of this experiment lead to her proposing that there are there are several types of attachment styles. These are:

Secure Attachment

This is an attachment where a child feels loved, safe, and secure. The primary caregiver is responsive to all the child's needs. The caregiver consistently meets their child's needs which forms the foundation of a trusting relationship. Children with this attachment will often feel safe to go and explore their environment.

The securely attached child is confident in their interactions. This child is thought to then be able to form long-lasting relationships with others.

Insecure Avoidant Attachment

In this attachment, a child may seem emotionally distant and avoids comfort from the primary caregiver. This insecure-avoidant attachment is where a child with an insecure-avoidant attachment is thought to have parents who are unresponsive to their needs.

The insecure anxious-ambivalent child may also be unsure of its caregivers and possibly distrusting. As a result, this child's insecurity may result in them being cautious in exploring their environment.

Insecure Ambivalent/Resistant Attachment

In this attachment style, the child may display clingy behaviour or be resistant to a caregiver's care and attention. This is due to the child's primary caregiver being inconsistent responding to the child's needs.

The insecure ambivalent/resistant child may also struggle to understand and express their feelings.

Disorganised Attachment

Children with this attachment style do not fit into the other styles outlined by Ainsworth.

Children with disorganised attachments may avoid or find relationships with others challenging.

Applying Theory to Professional Practice

Applying the work of Bowlby and Ainsworth requires you to reflect upon how you prepare children and their families to transit to your setting and form attachments to you, their caregiver, in the absence of their parents/carers.

As a humanistic practitioner, you become the primary caregiver for young children and provide them with a secure base from which to explore their environment. Applying attachment theory in your professional practice, requires you to be the child's reassurance, comfort and security. Each child will then form an attachment. Attachment theory leads us to believe that early attachments made between you and the child will shape the child's internal working model. The internal working model is the cognitive representation or template of the relationship between the child and the primary caregiver; in this instance, the primary caregiver is you – the humanistic practitioner.

Summarise This Theory in Your Reflective Journal and Apply to Your Professional Practice

Summarise your understanding of attachment theory. How does attachment theory apply to your professional practice? Take time to research further Bowlby and Ainsworth. Research and summarise Ainsworth's Strange Situation experiment.

Applying your critical thinking and analysis, how can you critique the work of Bowlby? Discuss.

How as a humanistic practitioner do you ensure every child as a secure base where they can return for comfort and reassurance? Give examples.

Professional Love and Relationships

Having explored humanistic and attachment theory, and considered how this theory applies to your professional practice, you may have heard of the term, 'key person'. A key person is the practitioner to whom that child is assigned and with whom they will possibly form their first attachment to. The key person is the humanistic practitioner who supports every child's transition and in particular the transition from their primary caregiver to you as their humanistic practitioner/key person.

As a humanistic practitioner, you need to consider how to apply humanistic and attachment theory and reflect upon how you will support every child to feel safe and secure and form secure attachments.

Being

A secure attachment which will enable every child to feel secure, confident, and empowered to explore their enabling environment.

Read my reflective account. This is an account of my days as a Nursery Nurse conducting home visits and forming initial bonds with my key children.

Reflective Account – Home Visits and First Relationships

In my Nursery Nurse days, I was key person for several children in my family group. These children were assigned to me prior to starting Nursery. I would make contact prior to the child starting Nursery and plan a home visit. This home visit was my first connection with the child and the start of our relationship. However, I devised a way to form an attachment and a bond with every child and this is what I would do.

On the home visit, I would take several toys, books, and the Nursery bear who incidentally would be travelling in the back of my car in its seat belt! (The things us Early Years practitioners do naturally.) However, the main thing I took was a set of Duplo bricks which I would use to try and encourage the child to build with me whilst in their home. I would sit and be guided by the child's play, talk to parents, and even have a cup of coffee with the family. I would gather information about the child's likes, dislikes, needs, and wishes.

Upon leaving, I would take one Duplo brick and give it to the child and ask them to please bring this one brick with them on their first day at Nursery as I would be waiting for them to play Duplo together.

The final thing I wish to share with you is that this little brick was saved from their first day and packed away in a box labelled with the child's name. The little brick in the box was saved for the duration of the time the child was in Nursery with me, and on the day they left, the box and little brick were given back to the child and their parents/carers as a goodbye but also as a symbolic representation that as a Nursery Nurse I hoped I had provided the child with a firm foundation, a secure base, an attachment, and a sprinkling of professional love to send them onto their next adventure.

 ## Reflective Questions

Reading my reflective account, can you see how I used this approach to create a bond, an attachment, and form a relationship with each child? Explain.

Can you make links to Bowlby's theory? How? Explain.

Has this reflective account inspired you? How will you support children transitioning from home to Nursery? Share your ideas with others.

Throughout your journey as a humanistic practitioner, you will support many children to transit from their parent/carers care to your setting. Each child will transit to a setting and form attachments

Being

differently. Every child is unique. For example, there will be children who will enter your setting ready to go and explore, whilst others will need more reassurance, but all children need your humanistic and professional love.

A humanistic practitioner continually displays professional love. Professional love is a term coined by Page (2018). Page defines professional love as the love and care a practitioner displays whilst the young child's parent/carer is absent. The professional love you might display are the hugs, the hand holding, the kind words you share, your facial expressions, the time and space you provide, alongside the safe arms and nurturing moments you offer a child.

Let's explore the term professional love with a reflective account.

Sarah is an experienced senior Early Years practitioner. In this reflective account, she shares her own perspective on professional love and how this relates to her key children.

Reflective Account – Professional Loving Relationship

I feel I have always had consistent loving and caring relationships with all my children which helps them to grow and thrive. I feel I can love and protect them and correct and guide them when needed.

I care for them when they are hurt, poorly, or upset.

I have strong feelings for my key children, love, concern, empathy, and frustration, just like a parent! I recognise my feelings.

I see my key children daily and I know them very well. Often my children are with me for a longer period than they are with their parents; this is a tough reality for parents. I must have empathy and understanding when communicating with these parents, they need to know I care, and they need to feel I care. As a key person, I feel my role compliments parenting, parents are secure in the knowledge that I care for their child, and to me, this is professional love.

To work with little ones, you need to feel warmth and compassion towards them; this should come naturally and cannot be forced, and it strengthens with experience. As your experience grows, you recognise this but also know how to remain professional and channel it into your practice and role.

 **<u>Reflective Questions</u>**

What professional values do you feel Sarah has shared in this reflective account?

Explain how she has displayed professional love and how she appreciates her parents/carers' emotions too?

Take some time to look back at your personal and professional values and answer how do these align to being a key person and a humanistic practitioner?

Planting your seeds of knowledge and understanding

At the end of this chapter, you are now ready to plant the seeds of knowledge you have discovered about humanism, attachment, and humanistic and attachment theory. You are now ready to reflect upon your understanding of how you will be a humanistic practitioner in your professional practice.

Take a moment to look back at the topics and using the image, reflect upon:

Describe humanism and how you apply humanism to your professional practice?

How do we form attachments with our young children and why is this important?

Reflecting upon the practitioner in the image:

How do you feel the practitioner is displaying professional love and humanism?

How do you know the young child in the umage feels secure, attached, and there is a connection between the key person and the child?

FIGURE 3.2 A practitioner holding a baby in her arms

4 The Observant Practitioner

In this chapter, you will explore the skill of observation and your role as an observant practitioner. You will be introduced to the different types of observations and the purpose of observations. You will also be encouraged to observe other professionals to develop your own observation skills.

The seeds of knowledge explored within the chapter are as follows:

Observation
Types of observation
Purpose of observation
Observe the observer observing

Observation

Observation is the act of watching something or someone closely, examining, and then commenting and reporting upon your findings. In early years, observation is the formal term for your daily monitoring of children's learning and development.

DOI: 10.4324/9781003361442-5

Recent changes in early years frameworks recognise that practitioners should not be spending time absorbed in conducting and compiling lengthy observations when they should be present and in the moment with children. Instead, practitioners should be focused on their engagement with the child, communicating and extending the child's holistic development. This level of engagement gives the practitioner the opportunity to focus more on enhancing children's play experiences, whilst still using their in the moment observations to inform future planning.

However, as a student practitioner, you are required to understand the many types of observation.

Types of Observation

There are several types of observations that you need to be aware of. These include the following:

Narrative Observation

This is a detailed observation. You may hear it referred to as a written record. This involves you observing and writing a detailed narrative of the child. You may only focus on one area of development as capturing specific detail in a narrative can be difficult. As this is a time-consuming approach, you may devise a code or some shorthand when recording this style of observation.

For example, I recall devising codes for the different types of play a child may be involved in to save me time when observing and recording.

Time Sample Observation

A time sample observation is an observation that you plan for a set period of time. For example, you might decide to take 30 minutes out of the day to observe a particular child every 5 minutes and record a child's engagement in the environment. It can provide you with a snapshot of a child's interests and disposition.

Tracking Observation

For this observation, you need to first produce a rough floor plan of your setting, inside and outdoors. You can then spend a period of time tracking a child's movements around the setting. This type of observation will show you a child's interests and their preferred resources. You can then use the data to inform your professional practice. In other words, you may find that you need to rearrange your provision if you observe a pattern where most children you observe using this method are not accessing a particular part of your provision.

Sociogram Observation

This is not a commonly used observation but one which can support you to identify a child's social interactions. In this observation type, you will choose a focus child and document their social interactions over a period of time. It will give you a picture of how the child develops socially.

Learning Stories

This type of observation is about building a story of a child. As an observant practitioner, you will be gathering evidence to put together the pages of a child's story. A learning story is a collection of photographs and/or pictures children have produced alongside your annotations. You will annotate what you have observed or even what the child may have told you about a particular picture they have produced, and you can add this to their learning story.

This learning story will document a child's interests, their likes and their engagement in activities and you can document areas of their development.

Post It Notes or Wow Moments

This is possibly the quickest type of observation, and whoever invented post it notes, I think you will come to thank them! You simply observe and capture a moment in time, a wow moment for the child where they have laughed, giggled, and achieved or persisted at an activity. These are quick and daily records of children and can be instantly shared with your colleagues and the child's parents/carers. Moreover, these wow moments add to a child's learning story.

Tapestry

You may be in a setting during your vocational training that uses tapestry. Tapestry is an online space that securely stores all your observations and annotations about children. It builds a picture of a child's learning and development and is shared between the setting and a child's parents/carers.

Ultimately, whatever type of observation you use, the aim is to capture a child's learning and development. It takes time to develop these skills, and each setting you work in will have their preferred method of observation. All observations conducted should be shared with the child's parents/carers and used to support children's next steps. Observations are powerful tools to be shared with external agencies if a child needs further support as well as for planning and assessment which we will also cover later in the chapter. However, observation is a skill, and we all develop this skill with experience.

Meesha is an experienced Early Years practitioner. She shares her experience and perspectives of developing her observation skills with her own key children. This account is open and honest and shows you that observation is a skill that develops with experience.

Read Meesha's reflective account.
Take time to reflect and answer the reflective questions.

Reflective Account – The Skill of Observation

I have learnt a lot about observing children over the years; I now understand that it is a skill that develops with time. Looking back, I remember how I always felt I needed a clip board, pen, and observation sheet to observe. I felt this was the right thing to do and the expected thing to do, and I guess these were my comfort 'tools' at that time. I began to realise as I reflected after each observation that they were very neatly written and repetitive and that something needed to change. It seemed that the observations were all about the pen and the paper, eyes down, missing quality moments. I knew the quality wasn't there. I knew I maybe had missed some wow moments in the child's learning and development.

As I became more experienced and confident in my practice, I started to relax. I began to tune into what children were saying, and I recognised spaces they preferred to play and chat in; these spaces were usually away from my watchful gaze. I listened and I really looked carefully, without pen or paper, and began to capture 'wow moments'. These moments offer a deeper connection into understanding their learning and motivators; this was being missed before. I felt inspired, and my confidence in my own practitioner knowledge grew.

I will share with you a quiet 'wow moment':

Two children were mixing paints together in the creative area, in a quiet corner. The rest of the group were all busy elsewhere. I approached the children and I said 'Light blue, white and a

little green makes turquoise, it's like the colour of the seaside'
both children agreed and continued to mix colours together.

They were both unaware I was observing them and more
importantly listening, knowing when to tune in and capture
that rich learning moment. I realised I had said enough and
did not need to say anything else to these two children.

I know I have gained confidence now, and I now trust my own
instinct, knowing where to be, look, listen, and when to commu-
nicate with the children. It isn't always the hustle and bustle areas
that provide the best opportunities for observation, you need to
look further than that: try and capture quieter moments too.

I enjoy observing so much more now, and I can finally
see the real value in observation. It is honestly more about
quality than quantity; I would much rather finish a busy
week with one rich captured observation or moment than a
pile of meaningless repetitive accounts.

It has been a journey for me, and it has not happened over-
night. I have had to take time to reflect and develop confi-
dence to get to this point, and I know the journey continues.

 **Reflective Questions**

Reflecting upon this account and having read the types of
observations, what do you feel the positives and negatives are
for observing children?

What do you feel the key message is from Meesha's account?
Explain.

Being

Developing your observation skills is something which takes time. However, you also need to be aware of how your observations inform planning and assessment.

Purpose of Observation

This chapter focuses on observation skills, but as an observant practitioner, you need to be aware of the purpose of observation.

As an observant practitioner, you will observe daily, and all observations are documented evidence of a child's learning and development. Observations are evidence of a child's achievements, their actions, and behaviours. Observations are a log of a child's developmental journey, and applying your knowledge of developmental milestones, you can then build a picture of what the child can do.

As you unpack each observation, use the information to include children in the next part of their journey. Try not to use observations as a sacrifice and an assessment which highlights what the child cannot do but to celebrate what the child can do.

Observations are used to inform planning and assessment but consider how you can include the child and the child's parents and carers in the co-construction of planning for the next steps of a child's learning and development. Observations are part of a range of documentation you will keep about a young child.

To develop your understanding of the purpose of observation, talk to your setting as to how they use their observation for planning and assessment.

Also, ask them how they might share their observations with parents/carers and any external agencies.

Observe the Observer Observing

Having explored different observation types and how these inform planning and assessment, I encourage you to observe the observer.

You are at the early stage of developing your observation skills, and it is a useful exercise to observe an experienced practitioner observing a child or a group of children or just observe a practitioner playing. Either one you choose will support you in your journey developing into an observant practitioner.

You can either:

Speak to a fellow practitioner and ask if you can observe them **observing** a child or a group of children. You can make your own notes as to what you have observed and then compare these with the observer. You will need the permission of the practitioner and the setting to conduct this observation, and this observation cannot be shared outside of the setting unless all ethical and full permissions are granted. After the observation, you can share your findings with the practitioner and have a professional discussion. This process will help you develop your observation skills and provide you with a different perspective of the child that the practitioner observed.

Speak to a fellow practitioner and ask them if you can observe them **playing** with a child or children. After the observation, you can share your findings with the practitioner and have a professional discussion. This process will help you develop your observation skills and provide you with different approaches to play that the practitioner you observed applied during the observation. Once again, this observation cannot be shared unless all permissions are granted by the practitioner and the setting.

Lucy is currently a Level 2 apprentice and developing her observational skills whilst studying for a Level 3 Early Years qualification. Lucy has shared her perspectives on observing the observer playing and interacting with children.

Read Lucy's reflective account and take time to answer the reflective questions.

Reflective Account – Observing the Observer

I had mixed feelings about participating in a peer observation. I don't mind being observed, but I just felt a little uncomfortable being observed by my senior colleague. The practitioner had invited me to observe a circle time session. She also asked me to observe and feedback how I felt the session went and talk about her professional practice. I thought, how can I comment on her practice, she is so amazing I don't have anything to say?

I closely observed, and I noticed details I had not noticed before. I noticed how she used body language and her hands to capture the children's interest and imagination. I listened to the tones in her voice, and I listened to how she pronounced words. I noticed the little things: how she quickly reacted to a situation with a child who struggles to listen. There were so many little discreet actions and interactions with the children that I had not noticed before. I remember thinking at the time, I will do that next time, that's a great idea!

It was an opportunity to pause and really observe what we do every day. I sit in circle time, and I don't always notice all the little things that happen. I think this is because the room is so busy, the day flies by and I am so involved with the children I don't always take time to stop and look. I am used to being observed as part of my training, I observe my key children daily, but I had never observed another practitioner. I shared my observation with my senior colleague, and we talked together about the experience; I felt comfortable doing this as I was eager to share what I had learned from the experience.

My colleague listened to me and thanked me for observing her; she shared she hadn't noticed how she uses her body language. We agreed that we would continue to observe each other and that it would be part of our Continuous Professional Development (CPD). I feel so much more confident about doing this now; it has now become normal practice in the preschool room; we shared this during a recent Ofsted inspection, I proudly told the inspector all about it!

 ### Reflective Questions

What did Lucy learn from observing the observer that she can take into her own professional practice?

Why do you feel Lucy was nervous about observing a more experienced practitioner?

What information did the experienced practitioner gain from being observed? Was this important for her future reflections?

How useful do you feel this exercise was and would you consider asking if you can observe the observer?

<u>Planting your seeds of knowledge and understanding</u>

At the end of this chapter, you are now ready to plant the seeds of knowledge you have discovered about the observant practitioner. You are now ready to reflect upon your understanding of how you will be an observant practitioner in your professional practice.

Take a moment to look back at the topics and using the image, reflect upon:

What is observation?

What are the different types of observation?

How are observations used?

How can you develop your observations skills? What support do you need?

How is the practitioner in the image using observations with parents/carers?

Why do we need to share observations?

FIGURE 4.1   A practitioner with two parents discussing their child's progress

Becoming

You need to train your eyes and your soul to reflect upon your perfectly imperfect self. You need to accept your inner beauty, appreciate your flaws and be courageous to seek out spaces where you can become your true self.

Annie Pendrey

DOI: 10.4324/9781003361442-6

5 | The Playful Practitioner

Play is an integral part of your professional practice. Play is a vehicle of learning and development for children. Play is a child's right. Play is also a vast topic, and as I wrote this chapter, I had to remind myself I was introducing you to the foundation of play. Therefore, this chapter is a starting point for your journey as a playful practitioner and not meant to be an exhaustive list of theories.

Instead, this chapter aims to scatter a few seeds of knowledge relating to play. It aims to ignite your curiosity and reflections. It aims to set you on the path of discovery and research. You can use the layout of each approach to play as a format for revision and to support you in your exploration and research around the topic of play and its many approaches as you grow in confidence and professional experience.

The seeds of knowledge explored within the chapter are as follows:

Play
Stages of play
Types of play
Approaches to play

DOI: 10.4324/9781003361442-7

Becoming

Play

Let's begin this chapter with defining the word play and considering what is play?

Journal Activity – What Is Play?

Think and answer what is play?

Research definitions of play.

Can you create a definition?

Share your definition with others. What is their definition of play? Is it similar to your definition? Does your definition need redefining?

Here are some of my definitions:

Play is the way children interact with their world. Play is intrinsically motivated. Play is engaging, stimulating, and fun. Play gives children the opportunity to explore and discover. Children learn and develop through play. Play has a meaningful value to children. Play is where children have space, freedom, and time. Play is a vehicle of learning. Play is universal, and as adults, we are fortunate to be invited to be a part of children's play.

Having defined what is play, it is important that you appreciate and understand that a playful practitioner has an important role in promoting children's holistic development. You have the privilege to be invited to enter the world of child's play. So, use this time carefully, reflect on your interactions, and use your reflections to develop your professional practice.

However, defining play is not enough to be a playful practitioner. You also need to understand about the stages of play, the types of play, the theory of play, and how play supports learning and development, some of which you will cover in this chapter. However, I would argue that before you can apply any of this knowledge, you must learn how to play. You must learn when children do not want you to play with them, and you must learn to sometimes join the child's play only when you are invited. You must also develop the knowledge and skills to appreciate each child is unique and their play journey will also be unique along with their learning and development.

Firstly, do you know how to play? I recall finding this very easy when I trained a Nursery Nurse (NNEB), and I believe this is because I had a much younger brother at home who I cared for after college whilst mom went to work and before dad came home from his shift in the factory. I started my course armed with some knowledge of how to play with at least one child. Of course, I went onto also learn that play is so much more!

So, I guess what I am saying is you might find it a little tough to know how to play when you start placement. Rest assured this is part of your learning process. My advice would be to sit alongside children to begin with, and believe me if they want to be involved in their play, they will tell you or they will offer you a toy, or if you are lucky, offer you a hat to pop on your head as they invite you to become part of their role play.

Equally, children may not invite you to play. It is in this moment, I encourage you to play alongside the children, create your own Lego house, pour yourself a cup of tea in the home corner, and lose your inhibitions. This includes chatting along to yourself, joining in singing, and reading stories. And oh, if you can't pronounce a word in a book, change the word or ask for help. I can honestly say, I have done all these things and subjected children to my horrendous singing voice, but children don't judge. Children love the fact that you are present, joining in, and having fun. As practitioners, we all have to learn to play.

Becoming

Megan is a student studying Level 2 in Early Years. She has shared her open and honest feelings about the beginning of her playful practitioner journey and how she had to learn to play.

Read Megan's reflective account. Take time to reflect and answer the reflective questions.

Reflective Account – Learning to Play

When I first started at Nursery, I was asked to play with the children with the cars and transport books. I panicked, as I didn't know what to say. There was only three children to play with, all of whom were toddlers.

I felt they wouldn't understand lots of questions and talking, so I just sat and watched them. I was gently told to engage with the children and talk to them and 'play'. I really wasn't sure how to, so I picked up the book and started to read to the children. I realised I was just reading to myself; they were not interested.

A staff member told me to turn the book around so that the children could see the pictures and engage. I knew that really and was embarrassed I hadn't done it; everyone was very kind and could see I was nervous. I was then told to just relax. It was suggested that I go and pick up a car and play myself which I did. I realised I was over thinking the whole situation.

I was making the play situation much more complicated than it needed to be, and I didn't need to. As soon as I picked up the car and started wheeling it around, the children started saying 'beep' beep'. I had been invited into their play. I then found it easier, and I began to read the books about cars, they looked at the pictures with me, we pushed our cars around together, and I really enjoyed it.

I will remember those early days; I can't believe I just sat there! I now find playing natural. I get straight in there now with any play experience now and have just as much fun as the children do!

This is a very honest and humble reflection. Megan relaxed and began to become playful and immediately the children became engaged as she had entered their world of play.

 ## Reflective Questions

Do you know how to play? Do others assume you know how to play?

Do you think playing and/or being invited to play by the children is a skill? Explain your thinking.

What is the importance of honesty and courage within this reflective account?

How has Megan's courageousness and honesty supported her journey as a playful practitioner?

Stages of Play

A playful practitioner needs to be aware of the stages of play. There are several stages of play as follows.

Becoming

Unoccupied Play (0–12 Months)

This is the foundation of play. This is where babies will gesture, make random movements, kick, wriggle, and wave their arms about as they interact with you and play.

Your role as a playful practitioner is to bond with the young child and give them the security to explore their environments and play. Babies, at this stage, may not be mobile, but they will use their eyes and gestures, and your role is to be responsive to their play needs.

Solitary Play (Zero to Two Years)

During this stage of play, young children will play alone. Children at this stage play alone and are happy to interact with resources and explore their environment alone.

Onlooker Play (18 Months – 2.5 Years)

During this stage of play, you will find children showing an interest in others play, but rather than being involved, they will be on the outside of the play, looking in. The child will be an onlooker, making mental notes and observing other children playing. They might play very close to the other children but not always join in.

Parallel Play (Two to Three Years)

This is where you might observe two children sitting alongside each other, and they may even be choosing similar toys. However, each child is only concerned with their own play. Their play is parallel as they may not wish to interact with the other child sat beside them.

Associative Play (Three to Four Years)

At this stage of play, children will become more interested in their peers. They begin to become more curious about other children and their play. Children at this stage of play will play with each other and even begin to choose the same toys or activities.

Co-Operative Play (Four to Five Years Plus)

In this final stage of play, children will not only begin to play with others but also as they play begin to define the rules of the play experience. Play becomes more sophisticated as the children play together with shared goals.

You can use these definitions of stages of play to inform your observations. You can begin to observe children in your professional practice/placement and consider what stage of play, you feel a child may be at a child is at.

You also need to consider your role as a playful practitioner supporting children's stages of play.

These include the following.

Creating Opportunities to Play

As a playful practitioner, you set the scene for children to play. You consider the likes of a child, the child's needs, the child's age, and stage of development. You can then begin to plan and create opportunities for the child to play. This might feel an overwhelming responsibility for you at first, but observe your peers, ask questions in placement about the stages of play, and seek support from your tutors. With time and experience, you will soon be a confident and experienced playful practitioner.

Observe, Support, Guide, and Accept Invitations

Use your observations to inform your playful practice. Observe each child's stage of play. Give each child time, and be there to support and guide the child's play. Be patient and let each child be curious, and accept any invitations to play with a child.

Types of Play

In addition to stages of play, there are types of play. As a playful practitioner, you need to provide children with different types of play to engage their interests and support their holistic development.

Each type of play will give the child an opportunity to learn and develop. Some types of play may develop one area of a child's development more than another. For example, block play might be considered to develop a child's physical development and as children bend, scoop, pick up, twist, and manipulate the blocks, that is most certainly physical play. However, this is not to say that physical play will only support physical development because during block play, a child may also communicate, verbally and non-verbally and socialise with others. So, it is important for you to be aware how the different types of play support a child's holistic development.

There are several types of play. Here are some definitions of types of play to support the start of your playful practitioner journey.

Physical Play

Physical play is the type of play that encourages children to move, be this hop, skip, jump, or run developing their gross motor skills. Physical play can also be when children are picking up a crayon, threading, or lacing. This is when children would be developing their fine motor skills. So, physical play can be a child using whole body movements and exerting energy or sitting quietly using only their arms and hands.

Creative Play

Creative play is a play experience that involves the child exploring, experimenting, and having the opportunity to engage their senses. Examples of creative play include, modelling, painting, drawing, dancing, and music.

Imaginative Play

Imaginative play is a play experience that sparks a child's imagination. For example, when a child plays with a puppet they will use their imagination and possibly give the puppet a name, a personality, and a life. Other examples of imaginative play include props and objects that will spark a child's imagination.

Sensory Play

This type of play is when resources and the play experience stimulates the child's touch, sight, hearing, taste, and smell.

Messy Play

Messy play is a play experience where the child is free to explore and discover the properties of materials such as sand, mud, and clay. Messy play is exactly that, messy! It is the type of play that you nor the children should ever wear your best clothes for.

Heuristic Play

Heuristic play is when children have the opportunity to play with and explore everyday objects such as wooden spoons, saucepans, and everyday objects that will stimulate the child's senses. All materials introduced to the child during this type of play need to be safe.

 **Journal Activity – Types of Play**

Having read the definitions of the types of play, it is a good time to add to your journal with some independent research.

Take time to look around your placement setting. Observe the different types of play. Take time to add to the brief definitions within the chapter.

Write a detailed description for each stage of play. Imagine you are describing a type of play to a parent/carer. How would you describe it to them?

Following your descriptions, now list some examples of each type of play. You can add to this after each placement experience.

How does each type of play support a child's holistic development? Be specific, consider how each type of play supports a child's physical, cognitive, communication and language, social and emotional development?

Reflect and discuss, what is your role as a playful practitioner providing the different types of play?

Challenge – consider how you can provide more types of play that are sustainable?

Approaches to Play

In addition to the stages of play, as a playful practitioner, you need to be aware of some of the key figures and approaches to play. There are many approaches to play, and this can be daunting as you start your career in the field of Early Years. Therefore, this chapter introduces you to a few approaches to play which I hope will support you in your professional practice. There are many more approaches to play, but I chose these particular approaches as I feel they will provide you with a strong foundation to continue your playful practitioner journey.

Use the overviews of each play approach to build your understanding of play. As you read each approach, consider how each the approach applies to your professional practice. You can then

. use the reflective questions at the end of each approach to journal your thoughts.

I hope that by engaging with approaches, will ignite your curiousuty and guide you to further research several more approaches to play.

Remember, this is the belonging part of the book and your journey, and so practicing what I preach, I hope that you find this a humanistic start to the approaches to play. And so, like a pick and mix bag of sweets, I choose a few key figures and approaches in the world of play for you to begin your understanding of play and its many approaches.

These include the following:

- Tina Bruce
- Elinor Goldschmeid
- Maria Montessori
- Forest School
- Highscope

Read each overview. Then take time to reflect and summarise each approach in your reflective journal. You can then research each key figure in more depth and adding your critical thinking and critical analysis when considering how each approach applies to your professional approach and pedagogical preferences.

You can then continue to use this format for other approaches to play for research and revision.

Overview – Tina Bruce

Tina Bruce's (2011) work is very much influenced by Froebel. One of the key elements of Bruce's theory is that play should be 'free flow'. Free flow is best described as the type of play where you will observe children totally absorbed, where they are setting their own agenda, making their own choices, and organising and developing their own rules.

Becoming

Your role within this type of play is to ensure that you provide the young child with the opportunities to move, to be free, and to have first-hand experiences. These opportunities allow the child to imagine, make choices, self-direct, and 'pretend'. Bruce talks about, 'personal play agenda', meaning every child should have the opportunity to be a child, to play with others or play alone. A personal play agenda is where a child can begin to think about their play and internally produce a script. A script is where the child might imagine, feel, and communicate their way through their play opportunity. As a Nursery Nurse, I used to imagine my children during free-flow play having their own internal dialogue and communicating to themselves their ideas, thoughts, feelings, and choices.

Your role as a playful practitioner encompassing Bruce's theory is to provide children with first-hand experiences and to observe play and take part in the child's play script once you are invited by the child. In other words, you follow the child's lead and do not lead or direct the child's play. Often as playful practitioners, we can become too enthusiastic and unknowingly control how children play. This is something you need to reflect upon as a playful and reflective practitioner.

Bruce also devised 12 stages of play. These are as follows:

1. Children need first-hand experiences.
2. Children create and make up rules regarding their play. That is, children can control their play.
3. Children symbolically represent as they play, for example children will adapt play props.
4. Children must have the choice to play. Children cannot be made to play. They must be in the mood to play.
5. Children role play. This means children pretend to be other people.
6. Children's pretend play is not necessarily children rehearsing and mapping out their future roles in society.
7. Children can play alone.

8. Children can play parallel to others or in groups.
9. Children have a play agenda, and children have a choice whether to share this agenda or not.
10. Children 'wallow' in their feelings during play.
11. Children display their competencies, their gifts, and skills during play.
12. Children coordinate their ideas and feelings, and this supports the child to bring together what they have learnt. This encompasses all aspects of a child's development.

Reflection

Consider how as a playful practitioner you can apply this approach to your professional practice.

Apply your critical thinking skills, what are the positives and negatives of this approach?

Do you apply all Bruce's 12 features of play in your professional practice? How? Explain.

Overview – Elinor Goldschmeid

The work of Elinor Goldschmeid (2004) introduces you to the words heuristic and heuristic play. Heuristic simply defined means 'hands on'. For you as a playful practitioner, this means providing children with objects that will give children the opportunity to explore, to have a hands-on approach to their learning.

Heuristic play is rooted in children's epistemic curiosity. If you recall, this is when children naturally want to be curious and wish to touch, feel, smell, lick, and bite objects, especially as a baby. Children are also curious to explore how objects react and how they can be manipulated. Having these opportunities will enhance many areas of a child's development.

As part of heuristic play, you may hear the term, 'treasure basket'. This is merely a basket of treasures such as natural materials like fir cones, pebbles, jam jar lids, and also lengths of ribbon and wooden spoons. All of these are treasures that children can explore whilst being uninterrupted by an adult.

Reflection

Consider how as a playful practitioner you can apply this approach to your professional practice.

Apply your critical thinking skills, what are the positives and negatives of this approach?

How as a playful practitioner can you provide an opportunity for heuristic play?

What areas of development do you feel a young child may develop during heuristic play? Explain.

Overview – Maria Montessori

Montessori is a widely used approach in Early Years education, and Maria Montessori's work stemmed from many studies and projects. One project was Casa dei Bambini. Casa dei Bambini is translated as Casa meaning home and bambini meaning children, so essentially children's home. Montessori set up Casa dei Bambini as a project for children who lived in disadvantaged areas, and practitioners employed there were guided by Montessori to engage child in play that was simple. This meant presenting children with simple objects to spark their imagination and for children to bask in their play experience.

Montessori also guided practitioners to utilise their observation skills and to provide children with the opportunities and experiences to use play. Montessori believed that practitioners should not hinder a child's sense of freedom, the freedom a child feels when immersed in their play experience. The practitioner should be an observant practitioner.

The observant and playful practitioner according to Montessori then creates an environment where children are free to enjoy long uninterrupted periods of play. Montessori was also prolific in introducing child-size furniture and equipment.

Montessori education is followed by many practitioners and settings. There may be some adaptations, but generally, Montessori education is based on three curriculum areas.

These include the following:

Care for the community
This is where children are encouraged to develop a sense of belonging and responsibility for their community.

Care for the environment
Montessori encourages children to develop a responsibility to care for their natural environment and their world. It encourages children to have a sense of responsibility towards sustainability.

Care for oneself
Montessori education encourages children to be independent and to develop their self-care skills.

Reflection

Consider how as a playful practitioner you can apply some this approach to your professional practice.

Apply your critical thinking skills, what are the positives and negatives of this approach?

Overview – Forest School

Forest school originated in Denmark and has become widely adopted in the UK. A forest school approach celebrates the integration of curriculum with the outdoors. Young children have continuous access to the outdoor environment, and practitioners ensure children have a sense of freedom.

Becoming

A forest school approach celebrates children taking risks with their learning. Practitioners supervise children in the open space to build dens, make fires, and be at one with nature and the great outdoors. There is a wealth of activities and types of play and areas of learning that can all take place using this approach; with the main emphasis being that children are immersed in nature.

Being immersed in nature gives children the opportunity to explore their senses, to feel a sense of freedom, independence, and engage in activities which promote problem solving, resilience, risk taking and much more.

Reflection

Consider how as a playful practitioner you can apply this approach to your professional practice.

Apply your critical thinking skills, what are the positives and negatives of this approach?

As a playful practitioner, imagine how many children may not have regular access to the outdoors and how important a forest school approach is for these children?

What activities could you provide that gives children access to the outdoors and follow the forest school approach?

List these activities. Explain what areas of development these activities will cover.

Overview – Highscope

Highscope was devised by Dr. David Weikart. Highscope was a result of many years of research and a response to low achievement of students in a state in the USA.

Its core principle are based on a wheel of learning, with the child at the centre.

The following explanations will support you in applying Highscope principles to your professional practice. These are described as follows.

Active Learning

Providing children with the opportunity for active learning, and time to reflect upon their experiences allows children to make sense of their world. As a playful practitioner you need to encourage to be curious, and to actively explore their world.

Key Experiences

The Highscope curriculum has 58 key developmental learning experiences. During these experiences, practitioners need to make anecdotal notes that inform their assessment and planning. This aligns to your work as an observant practitioner and a playful practitioner and how you might use observations to assess a child and inform your future planning.

Learning Environment

The learning environment includes setting up an environment that has appropriate resources, materials, and equipment for the child. An environment that empowers children to be autonomous, where every child can make their own choices and decisions.

The Daily Routine

A daily routine of consistency is considered to support a child's active learning.

Becoming

Plan-Do-Review

The final part of the wheel of learning is Plan-Do-Review. Supported by an adult, children plan what they would like to do, undertake the activity/experience, this is the doing. Children then review their learning experience. At this point, consider how you might review the experience with the child.

The infographic (Figure 5.1) shows how these principles are laid out in the Highscope wheel of learning.

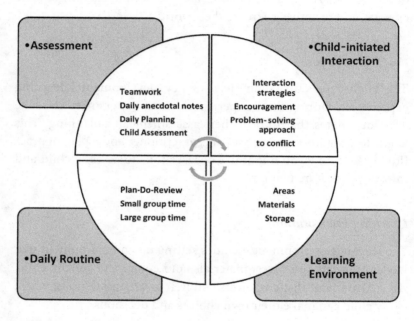

FIGURE 5.1 Highscope Principles

Reflection

Consider how as a playful practitioner you can apply some this approach to your professional practice.

Apply your critical thinking skills, what are the positives and negatives of this approach?

Are there any Highscope principles you need to research further? What are they?

Are there any Highscope principles you feel you already apply to your professional practice? What are they? Explain.

These approaches are just some of several approaches to play in Early Years and education but are a starting point for you as a playful practitioner. As you engage with more approaches to play throughout your studies and professional practice, you can continue to summarise each approach and reflect upon your role as a playful practitioner

You can also use the following journal activity to support your research, knowledge, and understanding of play.

Journal Activity – Observing Play and Approaches to Play

This is a lengthy journal activity, which has few questions but needs time spent reflecting and possible further research.

1. Using the pages of your journal, observe a child playing and note the following:

   What stage of play is the child at?

   Whilst observing this child, did you observe a particular approach to play? What was the approach? Explain.

   What could further enhance the child's play?

   What is my role as a playful practitioner?

Share your observations with your peers, mentor, assessor, tutor, and/or parents/carers.

2. Having been introduced to the different approaches to play. Summarise each one in your reflective journal.

   Carefully consider and reflect. How does each approach apply to your professional practice?

   Are there any approaches you prefer to others? Why is this?

   Can you critique some of the approaches? What are the positives and negatives of each approach?

   Have a professional discussion with your tutor, assessor, or peer about your critical reflections. What are their thoughts?

Finally, this book offers you only a brief overview of some of the approaches to play. There are many others. Take time to research and apply other approaches to your professional practice. Your tutor will support you with many other approaches to play.

<u>Planting your seeds of knowledge and understanding</u>

At the end of this chapter, you are now ready to plant the seeds of knowledge you have discovered about play. You are now ready to reflect upon your understanding of how you will be a playful practitioner in your professional practice.

Take a moment to look back at the topics and using the image, reflect upon the following:

What is play? How would you explain the importance of play to a child's parent/carer?

What is your role as a playful practitioner?

What are your reflections about the different approaches of play? Are there any approaches you wish to develop further as a playful practitioner? If so, how will you do this?

Finally, this is not a question but take time to observe play and consider what aspects of a particular play stage or approach you can see in action.

FIGURE 5.2   A practitioner and four children playing in a cardboard box

6 The Creative Practitioner

In this chapter, you will define the term creativity. You will also explore the range of qualities you need to be a creative practitioner as well as how to apply possibility thinking and the stages of creativity to your pedagogical approaches.

The seeds of knowledge you explored within this chapter are as follows:

Creativity
The qualities of a creative practitioner
Possibility thinking
Stages of creativity
The little pot of creativity

Let's begin this chapter with a journal activity.

DOI: 10.4324/9781003361442-8

Journal Activity

Using your reflective journal, define creativity.

Share your definitions with others.

Do you have similar words?

Produce a sentence that defines creativity.

How do you promote creativity in your role as a creative practitioner?

Creativity

My definition of creativity includes many words. I can honestly say defining creativity is not simple, and so, here is my definition. I believe creativity can only be defined using a multitude of words as creativity involves many key qualities. For me, creativity is about freedom and autonomy, having the freedom to explore and take risks. Creativity is about originality and uniqueness and as practitioners we should celebrate this.

Creativity is about beauty and imperfections, and if you have read any of my other books, you will know I talk a lot about **wabi-sabi,** which is simply defined as seeing the beauty in imperfection. Creativity gives you the opportunity to do this.

Creativity is also about imagination, and having the time and the space to reflect and spark your imagination and ideas. Creativity is a process and one not to be rushed. So, lets' stop the production lines of celebratory cards, and let every child feel freedom, explore their own ideas, use their imagination, and create something perfectly imperfect.

Stop for a while and reflect:

Reflective Questions

Reflecting upon your professional practice, how do you feel you create opportunities and provide an environment that encourages a child's creativity?

How do you ensure every child can be creative?

How do you ensure that every child has a sense of freedom?

Observe a fellow practitioner, and observe how they spark children's creativity and reflect upon your own practice. What have you observed?

How did that practitioner interact with the children? Is there anything you feel you need to develop about your own professional practice?

The Qualities of a Creative Practitioner

In this section, I want you to reflect upon how creativity is much more than the arts, the pots of paint and glue, and the hundreds of displays you will create during your career. A creative practitioner is much more than this. A creative practitioner is one who applies the following qualities to their observations, their planning and assessment, their pedagogical approaches, and their reflective practice. For example, one quality a creative practitioner must have is the ability to imagine and explore ideas. What I mean by this, is try not to continuously use social media and download ideas and then set out to reproduce them. Explore your own imagination, consider the likes, and needs of the children in your care, and more importantly, consider what will the child learn from the process?

Other qualities a creative practitioner should consider are as follows:

Experiment and Take Risks

A creative practitioner is a risk taker. Take risks in your pedagogical approaches, take risks in trying new things, and experiment. This is all part of your reflective journey. Step outside of your comfort zone. Be mindful that creativity does not mean you have to be able to draw, paint a watercolour, or produce a masterpiece from play dough! Creativity means experimenting and exploring different ways to support children's learning and development.

Face the Fear

A creative practitioner will face their fears and rise to a challenge. If you don't know how to do something, then don't be afraid to ask. I recall the first time I mixed powder paint, oh my! No one showed me how to do it, I was just sent to the art cupboard and told, 'Mix some paint'. Well, I stood ages staring at the powder and then the fun began. I mixed and wasted so powder paint in my first attempt. I produced coloured water, not colourful paint! I came to realise I had not added enough of the powder to the ratio of water. In addition, no one told me that when you open open each powder paint pot, they create this little cloud of coloured powder dust which goes all over you if you are not careful, and of course I was not careful. I can honestly tell you that I came out that cupboard sweating! Little did I realise that I would have to repeat the process again in the afternoon as I quickly began to discover children use lots of paint!

Becoming

Communicate, Observe, and Listen

This links to face the fear and my powder painting episode. I should have communicated to the reception teacher that I had never done this before, but I was too embarrassed, but then equally I also think the teacher could have shown me how to do it. Communication is key.

As a creative practitioner, you need to use communication as well as observation and listening skills to be able to stand back and observe the children in your setting. You need to observe children's creative interactions, listen to when they invite you to be part of their creativity, and communicate your observations to others in your team.

Work with Others

A creative practitioner needs to collaborate with others. This includes collaboration with your fellow practitioners to organise spaces and opportunities for creativity. You also need to collaborate with the children and their parents, this will help you discover a child's likes and dislikes and their interests. For example, do not assume all children will enjoy getting messy.

Be Resourceful

This quality makes me giggle because I know that now you have begun this Early Years journey and begin to consider the qualities of a creative practitioner, you will never look at a cardboard box, an empty egg box, or a pebble in the same way again. Trust me, you will begin to think, 'oh what can I do with that?' In today's world, we need to be more resourceful and kind to our environment. We need to think creatively but also about how we can be sustainable in our professional practice

Lisa, a Nursery Manager, shared with me her thoughts on being resourceful. She believes that as a creative practitioner you will soon begin to have a 'pocketful of treasures. I asked what she meant by this, and she explained:

> *Have you ever walked along a beach shoreline and noticed the tiny shells or shiny pebbles?*
>
> *Have you ever walked through a woodland or park and found pinecones or pieces of bark from an old tree?*
>
> *Have you ever become excited at the sight of a glossy mahogany brown conker peeping through a spikey green case?*
>
> *As a creative and resourceful practitioner, you might answer these questions with a yes. But Lisa then reminds us that, 'all these finds are a creative practitioner's treasure, they are lying there waiting to be found and taken to their next adventure. However, as an Early Years practitioner, we all need to be mindful not to take more than we need, or any at all as we need to respect the environment and natural habitats'.*
>
> *So, whilst you do need to be resourceful, you also need to be respectful, thoughtful, and sustainable.*
>
> *All these qualities will serve you well as a creative practitioner. Consider how you will demonstrate these qualities as you provide the children with opportunities to imagine, create, explore, and experiment. Reflect upon how you will observe and listen to children's creative ideas and be prepared to be wrong, especially when you tell a child that you love the snake they have just painted and they firstly look at you puzzled and then go on to say, 'it's not a snake, it's a worm!'.*

Possibility Thinking

Possibility thinking is a term coined by Craft (2000). Possibility thinking is the freedom to think of other possibilities. Possibility thinking is where questions such as 'what if' and 'why' arise from opportunities and experiences. Let me give an example from my own child, who I believe was born talking. I joke, but I do believe that my Early Years background ensured that my own children were surrounded with creativity but also given a space to exercise their possibility thinking.

A specific example of possibility thinking is one of my own lived experiences between my daughter and I. My daughter was about three years of age, and we were in the kitchen. Now this kitchen had the most horrendous wallpaper which we had inherited from the previous owners. We could not afford to change the wallpaper, so I decided, much to my husband's horror, that this wall would be my children's creative wall.

So, one day, my daughter was happily drawing on the creative wall, what I thought was a snake.

Me: I love your snake.

Rosie: Why?

Me: I love how it is all curly and is now sitting on our wall.

Rosie: Why do you think it's a snake mommy? It's a worm! Can't you see it's a worm?

Me: Sorry

Rosie: It's ok Mommy. If you don't know what it is again ask me! I can tell you; I have lots of ideas.

(Me and my inner voice, 'well, that's me told!')

This is a simple example and the start of possibility thinking. It shows how as a mommy and a Nursery Nurse I was fostering possibility thinking. A child's drawing on the wall or on paper can be anything the child wants it to be, but as practitioners, we need to engage with the child and encourage their possibility thinking. As a mommy, I then went on to extend this possibility thinking by asking Rosie questions such as, 'what if?' 'What if the worm was a snake?' 'What if the worm was to come alive?'.

The point is, that as a creative practitioner, you can provide a wealth of experiences and opportunities that promotes possibility thinking. Possibility thinking may occur naturally for some children, whilst other children might need your support to ignite their creativity and thinking.

Stages of Creativity

In addition to possibility thinking, Anna Craft (2000) describes creativity as a cycle. She believes that as creative practitioners, we can apply the five stages in her creative cycle as we consider the spaces and opportunities we provide.

Craft's five stages are described as follows.

Preparation

This stage is where the young child is present in a space, both physically and mentally, where creativity can take place.

Letting Go

In this stage, the child makes use of the space and can release their creativity. They can express themselves; they can let go and feel freedom.

Germination

Germination is where the child then begins to play out ideas, where they are filled with joy and excitement.

Assimilation

This stage happens over time. Craft (2000) believes that this is an internal stage where ideas may sit for a while and gestate. I envisage this stage as that trial and error, experimentation stage, and links to why we must give children time and space and the opportunity to revisit the roots of their idea.

Becoming

Completion

The final stage is completion. This is where the young child brings all their ideas, experimentation, imagination, and creativity together.

The Little Pot of Creativity

There are a range of activities associated with creativity. It is important to explore how creativity is not limited to painting, drawing, sand, water play, or play dough. Creativity is much more than these examples, and as a creative practitioner, you need to think creatively. You need to consider how creativity is stimulated through other play opportunities. You need to consider how creative you are in your pedagogical approaches.

I propose that every creative opportunity and experience begins as a seed, an idea that you or a child may have. But the seed alone will not flourish and bloom without some support. Try applying the four stages of my pot of creativity next time you begin to plan an idea or activity for young children.

The four stages are:

The Seed

This is your initial idea, the seed.

Germination

Share and germinate your idea with your peers, colleagues, tutor, and the children. Children will give you their honest feedback. Germinating and sharing your ideas is a reflective process. You will gain a different perspective from others about your idea, which you can use to make amendments to your original idea (the seed).

At the germination stage, you could also consider Hart's Ladder of Participation covered in Chapter 1 as well as taking time to reflect upon your idea (your seed) supports a child's holistic development. Once germination is complete, you are ready to watch your seed grow.

Growth

Put your creative idea into action. Undertake the activity/experience and observe the child. Listen to their interactions. Communicate with the child but also be prepared to step back and let them have a sense of freedom. Bruce (2011) calls this cultivating creativity.

Bloom

At this stage in the pot of creativity, the child should bloom. You can use your observation skills to assess the impact the creative activity/experience has had upon the child. You should have observed the child experimenting, engaging, and exploring. Moreover, you should have been able to observe and note how the experience has impacted upon the child's holistic development.

If your original idea (the seed) did not germinate and bloom, then it's simply time for some repotting. Not every idea you have will be successful and that's part of your professional development. You must be resilient and keep planting new seeds of creativity.

FIGURE 6.1   A plant pot and two flowers

Planting your seeds of knowledge and understanding

At the end of this chapter, you are now ready to plant the seeds of knowledge you have discovered about creativity, the qualities of a creative practitioner, possibility thinking, and the stages of creativity.

You are now ready to reflect upon your understanding of how you will be a creative practitioner in your professional practice.

Take a moment to look back at the topics and using the image, reflect upon:

What is creativity?

What is possibility thinking?

How can you apply the little pot of creativity to your next creative activities/experiences with children?

Using the image below, how has the creative practitioner supported this young child's creativity?

What areas of development do you feel the activity in the image covers? Do you feel the practitioner encouraged possibility thinking during this activity?

FIGURE 6.2   A babies feet in sand and water

7 | The Inclusive Practitioner

This chapter forms part of the theme **BELONGING**. As part of the belonging theme, you will have the opportunity to reflect upon your professional values. You will be able to use the contents of this chapter to reflect upon how you will ensure that every child in your care feels a sense of belonging in their environments, an environment that gives them the security, love, and the autonomy to access a full range of opportunities to develop and thrive.

As part of your role in Early Years, you will need to reflect upon your role in providing environments that are inclusive, and how you ensure equality of opportunity for all.

The seeds of knowledge explored within the chapter are as follows:

Terminology and acronyms
Personal Values
Professional Values
Putting Values into action
Espoused and Enacted Values
Models of ability not disability
Legislation, Frameworks, Policies and Procedures
Children's Rights

    DOI: 10.4324/9781003361442-9

Terminology and Acronyms

Terminology and acronyms are used a lot in the world of education, and often it is assumed that we all understand their meanings. However, from personal experiences, I have often been in meetings where an acronym has been used and I have been unaware of it. Of course, I would advise you to instantly query what any acronym stands for, if you were to face this situation. However, for a variety of reasons, be it fear, embarrassment, or lack of confidence, as professionals we may not do this. Take time here to consider how parents and carers must feel in our educative world of acronyms and definitions, and so with this in mind, it is important that in our role as practitioners, we support or families to fully understand the many acronyms of education.

 **Journal Activity – Acronyms**

Let's begin this chapter with a journal activity. This activity will support you with the terminology and acronyms that are used in our education system, particularly related to inclusion.

Below are just a few of many acronyms that you may encounter as part of your professional journey. Take time to answer and define the terms and acronyms. Be honest. If you do not know them, don't look at the back of the book for the answers!

The point of the exercise is to build upon your knowledge and understanding of acronyms. You will observe them in use in your professional practice. You will go on to critically reflect upon their meaning and application to your work in Early Years.

- ADD
- ADHD
- ASD
- EHCP
- EP
- ESOL
- IBP
- IEP
- PECS
- SENCO
- SEN
- SLCN
- SpLD
- TAC
- VI

Next add any acronyms that are not on the list but you are aware of.

You can add to this list at any time during your studies. Finally, let me repeat and advise you to ask immediately if someone uses an acronym you don't understand. Join the educative world of acronyms!

Personal Values

Values are the long-lasting beliefs that are important to you as an individual. Your personal values become the standards by which you live your life and conduct yourself personally and professionally.

It is worth reflecting upon that at some point both your personal and professional values may be tested during your Early Years career, especially if they are misaligned to an ethos or institutions' values.

In this chapter, you will explore your personal values and professional values. Moreover, you will reflect upon how you display your values as an Inclusive Early Years practitioner.

Before we begin to explore what our professional values, let us pause and take time to consider what are our personal values and where these might stem from?

 **Reflective Questions**

Where do you believe your values came from?

Can you honestly say you are true to your personal values in all situations?

Has there been a time when your personal values may have been challenged and how did you feel?

 Journal Activity – Personal Values

Using the blank infographic, take time to consider what are your personal values?

Becoming

Write each of your personal values inside each circle and add more circles and values as you reflect upon your personal values.

Finally, what do you feel are your top three personal values and why have you chosen these three?

How do these link to your role as a practitioner?

A list of personal values can be found at the back of the book.

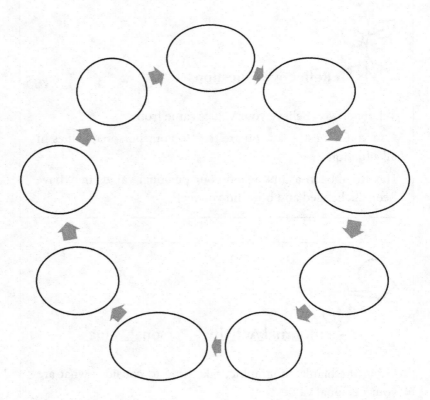

FIGURE 7.1 A cycle of circles with no text

Professional Values

Entering any career within education, you will be introduced to a set of professional standards that your educative sector or employee will expect you to display, and the field of Early Years is no different. Below is a brief collection of professional values. These are essential values for you to consider and reflect upon as you develop and progress in your Early Years career.

This collection of professional values is not exhaustive; there are many more professional values which you can reflect upon, define, and apply as part of your role as an Early Years practitioner.

Here are a few professional values briefly defined for you.

Empathy

Empathy is the ability to appreciate and share the feelings of others.

Confidence

Confidence is part of your self-belief. Confidence is the feeling that you have the ability to attempt something, go somewhere, or ask someone a question for example. Confidence is something you can develop and you will do so as part of this learning journey.

Patience

Patience is the ability to accept, tolerate, and appreciate others and their feelings and opinions.

Passionate

Being passionate is important. You can display your passion in many ways, such as continuing to extend your subject knowledge and develop your skills.

Becoming

Courageous

Being courageous is having the ability to face your inner fears. It is your ability to try and not be afraid to make mistakes.

Positivity

Positivity is the ability to stay optimistic and hopeful in adversity.

Knowledge and Inclusion

Knowledge and inclusion are a further two values you may feel form part of your professional values. However, knowledge is ongoing, so engage in as many professional development opportunities in order to develop your inclusive practice.

 Reflective Questions

Now stop and look back at your personal values and reflect upon how they might match your professional values.

Why should we reflect upon our personal and professional values?

Are there any professional values you feel you need to develop? How will you do this?

Journal Activity – Values

Using the blank infographic to log your values. Add more circles and values as you reflect and continue on your Early Years journey.

Finally, what do you feel are your top three professional values and why have you chosen these three?

How do your top three values align to your role as an Early Years practitioner? How will you display these professional values in your work with young children and their families?

There is a list of professional values at the back of the book.

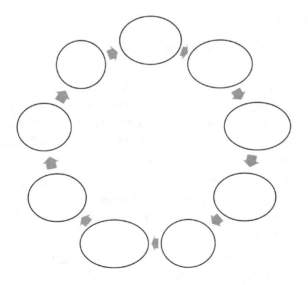

FIGURE 7.2 A cycle of circles with no text

Putting Values into Action

Reflecting upon your personal and professional values is an excellent starting point in considering who you are as an Inclusive Practitioner. Remember that your values may be compromised or challenged within your professional practice. However, you need to remember that you are an advocate, a reflective activist, and you must voice your opinions and concerns if your values are challenged. The point is, now you have identified your personal and professional values, it is time to put them into action!

Let's begin with a reflective account.

Parents with children with different abilities often face challenges. Read the reflective account from Maya, a mother and advocate of inclusion, as she shares one of her lived experiences.

 Reflective Account

Maya is a proud mother of three Scottish Jamarians (mixed Jamaican-Bulgarian roots), of which one child received a diagnosis of Down's Syndrome. Maya has had a career as a legal executive, has an MA in International Relations and Law, and is currently a freelance interpreter.

She kindly shared with me in an informal chat that her child's diagnosis was a blessing as it broadened her perspectives on many issues people with disabilities face daily. These words are wrote by Maya.

Read Maya's reflective account and then pause to reflect and answer the reflective questions.

Picture Inclusion – the opposite of having someone 'invisible' in a group

It was my second birth. But my son's arrival was not greeted with ooohs and awws. He was not deemed cute or 'perfect' and the silence preceding his diagnosis of Down's syndrome lay heavy. The midwife declined to weigh him immediately advising me to just enjoy him a bit. There were no 'congratulations' and 'all the best's' greetings; we were told to leave whenever we wished and no need to announce ourselves. Quietly and silently, we tried to adjust to this different treatment.

During the Primary school years, we tried to fit in. I recall my son sitting on the floor refusing to go into school, bodies zooming, some trampling over us. A child slows down, holds out her little hand and says: 'Come, Dillan'; he takes her words in and just when he is about to react and tries to swivel onto his knees, the little girl is jerked back by her mum: 'come on now, Zoe*, we don't want to be late'. My son sits back confused and watches his friend disappear inside.

I also recall times of laughing with parents by the school gate until the topic turns to homework., Maths, and after-school clubs, all the things that my son is not part of. As opinions arouse emotive voices around me, I quietly and silently retreat.

Primary school failed to make this one reasonable adjustment – have a designated person assist our son. Instead, they juggle him, toss him around like a hot potato, and insist he is 'coping well'. We write and we speak, and we insist: his sister is there as are all the little friends he has ever had. Dillan seemed permanently unsettled. But school said they had not been successful in finding the right person to support him, so the juggling continues and Dillan's reluctance to go becomes unmanageable. At age eight, I could no longer lift him and carry him in, and being pregnant certainly does not land well with such task nor does his ability to wilfully triple his body weight. He is not taken to trips out as 'it is not fair on the other children, what if he was to refuse to walk on'. Wolves have got this figured out, the slowest and the most infirm set the pace of the pack.

We take Dillan out of mainstream, away from the children whose life he is making difficult. He is silent and quiet but occasionally asks where his big sister is. Some parents get it and cry at the injustices with me, and others try to console me by saying that it is 'better for him'. I silently scream and retreat. There is simply no point trying to explain something to people who already understand it well.

My friend's daughter has Down's syndrome. She loves children, any age, and tries to make friends by saying 'Hello'. They are having lunch at their favourite restaurant and K is repeatedly trying to get the attention of the children on nearby table. The children seem intrigued, but parents insist on teaching them good manners which involve repeatedly ordering their offspring to 'just ignore' K. She initially greets them louder, changes greeting to Hiya, and eventually retreats in her seat, quiet.

We seek our tribe now, we seek a tribe of people who get us! These are usually the people who have had first-hand POSITIVE experiences with disability, not the people who feel sorry for us, but the people who see us, hear us, and want to know all about us.

Reflective Questions

What are your reflections from this account?

How has reading this account made you feel?

Can you align your feelings to any of your personal and professional values?

What do you feel your role is as an inclusive practitioner to ensure acceptance?

Can you define inclusion?

Chat to a peer, what is inclusion and equality?

Espoused and Enacted Values

In addition, to your personal and professional values, there are espoused and enacted values.

Espoused values are values that an organisation or person believes in and are the desired values of that person or organisation. The organisation here may be your workplace or placement setting. In organisations, the values are often seen in their mission statements or ethos. For example, a school may have something simple such as, 'Be extraordinary'.

Enacted values are the values that you and others perceive to be valued by the organisation. An example of this is where the organisation may have core values of empowerment and dignity and worth, but as a practitioner, you may not feel empowered.

Becoming

Finding an organisation that is aligned to your values is an excellent foundation for your career.

Now is an excellent opportunity to reflect upon your personal, professional, espoused, and enacted values.

Journal Activity – My Lantern

Copy the lantern or draw your own in your journal.

1. **The Flame**. Your lantern must have a flame. The flame represents your values. Choose four of your values that you feel are important to you? These are the values that light your way in your role as an inclusive practitioner.
2. **Protect the Flame.** All lanterns have devices that protect the flame. As an inclusive practitioner, you also need to protect your flame. Surrounding yourself with people and working within organisations that align to your values will protect your flame.
3. **The Handle**. There will be times in our professional carrier when we struggle or feel overwhelmed. This is when we should maybe pick up our lantern and walk away from the situation for a while. The handle represents how we need to identify and reflect upon any behaviours or situations which may dim our flame (our values). Here you can reflect upon the following statement, I know I'm out of alignment with my values when ....

4. **The Base.** On the base of your lantern, it is important to stop and be aware of your support network. Who is in your support network? Take time to think who these people are and how they can support you.

5. **Radiate Light.** Having reflected upon all the parts of your lantern. It is now time to consider how you will apply all your values to radiate light. How will you reflect light? How will you shine a light on equality and inclusion in your professional practice?

FIGURE 7.3 An outline of a lantern

Models of Ability Not Disability

As a Nursery Nurse and a mother, I have my own personal accounts of Special Educational Needs, and so, this chapter has been written from my head and my heart. In this section, you will be introduced to what is often referred to as models of disability.

You need an awareness of these models for your professional practice, but I would encourage you to reflect upon the ability of all children. You need to promote children's rights; you need to be an advocate and celebrate ability!

Disability is considered to have different models. These models are approaches to how society may view disability. There are two main models to be aware of and these are described as follows:

The Medical Model

The medical model is where a person's disability is viewed as a term, a difficulty, or an aspect of their medical condition. This model emphasises the diagnosis of a person's disability, impairment, or health condition. Assumptions may be made, and labels attached to a person's disability as opposed to their ability.

The Social Model

The social model offers a different perspective. Rather than viewing the person's disability, it looks at how the disability is just a part of the person, a characteristic, and it is societies' attitudes, acceptance, understanding, and creation of societal barriers that fail to ensure inclusion.

This is the tip of the inclusion iceberg, but it does lead you to reflect upon the language we use in our society such as disability and impairment. As a society and as an inclusive practitioner, you have a duty to promote children's rights and to challenge discrimination using legislation, frameworks, policies, and procedures to support you.

Legislation, Frameworks, Policies, and Procedures

There is a wealth of legislation and frameworks that aim to protect the rights of a child. Legislation is a law passed by parliament.

Legislation and frameworks inform organisations policies and procedures. A policy is a statement of intent, and procedures are implemented by you, the practitioners.

You need to be aware of and update yourself continuously of all current legislation, and frameworks and understand how these impact upon your role as an inclusive practitioner.

The aim of this chapter is not to list endless legislation and frameworks but to highlight the importance of keeping yourself updated and to appreciate how legislation and frameworks impact upon your practice. Equally, you will have the opportunity to reflect upon how your personal and professional values when promoting the rights of the child.

So, let's begin to consider how legislation, frameworks, policies, and procedures are connected and how they inform your professional practice. If you think of them as a kind of flow chart, this will help you understand the process. You play an integral role in following policies and implementing the procedures.

FIGURE 7.4 A series of rectangles and circles connecting legislation and frameworks to policies and procedures

Using the flow chart, let's examine how this might be applied to your professional practice. This is just one example.

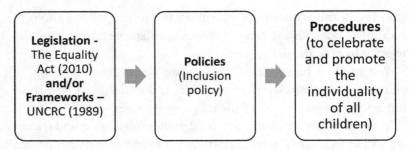

FIGURE 7.5 Three rectangles connecting the Equality Act and UNCRC to policies and procedures

Your organisation must follow the law. Your organisation will interact with both legislation and frameworks. For example, an inclusion policy derives from the Equality Act (2010). You may have already been given a set of policies to read from your setting, or if you are about to commence a setting, or a new job, you should try to access their policies which are usually on their intranet.

Each policy, in this case the inclusion policy, will set out several procedures. These are essentially statements which as a practitioner you should follow. Following these procedures will ensure every child has their rights met.

Take some time now to research and read key legislation, frameworks, policies, and the procedures you should be following as an Early Years practitioner. Maybe, you could begin with legislation that relates to inclusion.

The Equality Act (2010)

The Equality Act (2010) is designed to address the inequality and discrimination that certain people or groups face in our society. As an inclusive practitioner, you are responsible for addressing inequality, promoting opportunities, and reacting to discrimination.

The Equality Act (2010) may have terminology that is new to you as a practitioner. It is essential you understand this terminology and apply it to your professional practice. So, it's time to research. Grab your journal.

Journal Activity - Research, Define, and Reflect

What are the key characteristics of the Equality Act?

What is direct discrimination? Can you give an example of direct discrimination?

What is indirect discrimination? Give an example of indirect discrimination?

What are the procedures for addressing and dealing with discrimination in your setting?

United Nations Convention for the Rights of the Child (1989)

The UNCRC (1989) is a framework. It has 54 articles and protects the rights of children and young people up to 18 years of age across the world. Articles 1–41 examine how children and young people should be treated so they are safe, healthy, happy, and achieving. It is your role as an inclusive practitioner to ensure every child's rights are met.

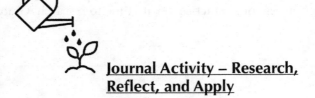

Journal Activity – Research, Reflect, and Apply

Research and read UNCRC (1989)

List the articles.
Choose five of the articles. List these in your journal.
Now reflect and scribe how you ensure each of these children's rights are promoted.

Give some specific examples.

What improvements could be made to not only your professional practice but also maybe by your institution and the wider society to promote children's rights?

Remember, this is not an exhaustive list of legislation and frameworks. It is merely the beginning of raising your awareness of legislation and frameworks and how you will apply these to your professional practice to be an advocate for children's rights. Continue using your journal to research, reflect, and apply other key legislation and frameworks to your role as an inclusive practitioner.

Children's Rights

In Chapter 8, you will be introduced to reflection and reflective activism. Once you have read this chapter, I believe you will begin to consider how you can be a reflective activist as well as an inclusive practitioner, particularly when promoting children's rights.

Your awareness of direct and indirect discrimination interspersed with your observation skills is one way of promoting children's rights. In a world where we are often judged for our looks or abilities, the inclusive practitioner plays an important role in eradicating the labels that society bestows on certain groups and individuals.

To summarise, the inclusive practitioner needs to ensure opportunity for all. Your work will involve providing accessibility to opportunities, celebrating difference, uniqueness, and valuing diversity.

You will be aware of and apply key legislation, frameworks, and policies to your professional practice.

Having researched both the Equality Act (2010) and UNCRC (1989), complete the following journal activity.

 ## Journal Activity – Capturing the Be (Bee) Moments

In this journal activity, you will reflect and explore how as an inclusive practitioner, you will provide opportunities for children to belong, become and thrive.

To be given the opportunities to **belong.**
To be given the opportunities to **become.**
To be given the opportunities to **thrive.**

Choose a case study, a child or group of children, or an oppressed group as your focus for this activity. You could use Maya's reflective account.

What are the challenges for your case study child or group?

Why do you feel every child needs to feel a sense of belonging and inclusion?

What reasonable adjustments are needed to ensure every child/group belongs, becomes, and thrives?

What are the challenges and how will you overcome these?

What aspects of the Equality Act (2010) do you feel applies to your child or group?

Explain how you will provide opportunities that ensure that reasonable adjustments are made for the child to achieve and thrive?

Which UNCRC articles align to your case study child or group?

Explain how you will provide opportunities that ensure the UNCRC articles you have chosen are embedded within the opportunities for the child/group?

Challenge – As an inclusive practitioner, are there any possible conflict with your values as you ensure this or other children, belong, become, and thrive?

FIGURE 7.6 An outline of a bee

Reflective Questions

How do we support our children and young people to move from being to becoming to thriving?

Do we have a world, a society, and structures that support our children and young people's thriving?

Planting your seeds of knowledge and understanding

At the end of this chapter, you are now ready to plant the seeds of knowledge you have discovered about inclusion, legislation, frameworks, and policies.

You are now ready to reflect upon your understanding of how you will be an inclusive practitioner in your professional practice.

Take a moment to look back at the topics and using the image, reflect upon:

What is inclusion?

Can you explain what is legislation, a framework, and a policy and how these apply to your role as an inclusive practitioner?

What are the rights of a child?

From your reading, reflect and answer the following questions:

I feel …
I appreciate …
I wish …
I view …
I need …

A further reflection and challenge:

Use this image to reflect upon the key terms in each circle and maybe add a short reflection to your journal. How will ensure you display all these key terms in your work as a practitioner?

FIGURE 7.7   A cycle with five circles outlining elements of the inclusive practitioner

Use this image to discuss with others, reflect, and consider what do all children need to thrive.

There are some key words in the image to prompt your reflections.

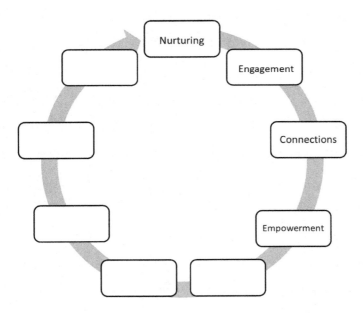

FIGURE 7.8 A circle of rectangles with arrows connecting the rectangles. Four rectangles have some key words as prompts for your reflection as to what a child needs to thrive.

Thriving

When things get tough, turn your face towards the sun. You will develop and thrive at your own pace. Be prepared to bloom.

Annie Pendrey

DOI: 10.4324/9781003361442-10

8 The Reflective Practitioner

In this chapter, you will begin to see and feel how the reflective nature of this chapter will lead you to reflect upon things from previous chapters. For example, as you begin to consider what is reflection, you will begin to appreciate the importance of being curious in Chapter 1.

This chapter is aimed at shining a light on your reflective practice and aims to support you to look for those shiny moments of your professional practice. As you progress from being, to becoming to thriving. The topics you will explore include: reflective practice, and activism as well as several theorists and models of reflection.

The seeds of knowledge explored within the chapter are as follows:

Starting your reflective journey
Barriers to reflection
Reflective practice
Reflective activism
Reflective theory
Reflective writing

DOI: 10.4324/9781003361442-11

Starting your Reflective Journey

Reflection is very much related to being curious. It requires you to be curious and reflective about yourself as an individual and as an Early Years practitioner.

Reflection is about detangling, detangling your own and other perspectives about a situation, an activity, or your professional practice. If you like, think about reflection like a bowl of spaghetti. When you look at spaghetti in a bowl, you will see it knots and entangles; it seems to have no starting or end point. Reflection can be viewed very much the same. It is a never-ending series of knots, twists, and turns.

This chapter is aimed at shining a light on your professional. This chapter will support you to search for those shiny moments within your journey from being to becoming and thriving. You will be encouraged to use your reflective journal to capture your reflections. I also encourage you to continually revisit your reflective journal So that you can reflect back upon your progress.

Let's begin with your first journal activity.

Journal Activity – I am

Let's start this reflective journey with a journal activity. This reflective activity is about beginning your journey of self-discovery. To identify who you think you are as an individual. You can approach this activity in several ways.

First, copy the sunflower image into your journal. Place the word I in the centre of the flower.

FIGURE 8.1   A sunflower outline

Now begin to think about who you are. You need to complete
   the sentence **I am ....**

For example, I am unique. I am creative and so on. Write
   your responses to the following statements on each of the
   petals.

Here are some descriptive words that might describe you:

Creative, confident, quiet, inquisitive, organised, stressed,
   reflective, caring, inspirational, enthusiastic, dedicated,
   disorganised, thoughtful, empathetic, loud, bossy, with-
   drawn and logical.

   Please think and add more words that you feel best describes
you.

Using this activity now reflect upon and answer the following
questions

Why are the adjectives you have identified important to the
role of an Early Years practitioner? Explain your thinking.

Share your collection of words with a peer. Discuss.

Have you identified some adjectives that you feel describe you as an individual but are not transferable to your role as an Early Years practitioner?

Challenge yourself and continue this reflective activity and complete the following statements:

I wish ....

I imagine ....

I believe ....

This journal activity is the start of your journey of self-discovery. The beginning of your awareness in deciding what matters to you and how you align what matters to you in your personal and professional. Self-discovery helps you accept yourself, appreciate your emotions, and supports your relationship with others.

Self-discovery involves five Ps. These are as follows:

Personal. Remember that your reflective journey of self-discovery is personal. You are unique, so do not compare your academic, reflective, and professional journey to that of others.

Purposeful. As you spend more time discovering yourself and reflecting upon who you are as an individual and as a professional, you will discover your sense of purpose.

Present. This means not thinking and reflecting too far ahead but being present in the moment, in the here and now. Self-discovery is a process not to be rushed.

Priorities. Being self-aware and taking time to reflect will give you the opportunity to consider and set your priorities for your studies and career. Share these priorities with your supportive network.

Perfectly imperfect. Appreciate that you are YOU! Appreciate we all make mistakes. Appreciate we are not perfect, and we should accept ourselves for who we are today and reflect upon who we might be tomorrow, possibly always perfectly imperfect!

As mentioned earlier, you can imagine reflection like a bowl of spaghetti; it twists, turns, and spirals. It should be regarded as a never-ending process. If you like, you can also imagine it as a movie that has a cliff hanger ending, the type of movie that never quite ends as you imagine, and you are left wondering what the ending might be.

However, in this particular movie, the main character is you!. There are other characters in this movie such as your mentor, peers, colleagues, children, families, community, legislation, theory, and literature. Each of these characters has a part to play, and they may all appear at different times in your reflections. And just like characters in a movie, there may be characters you like and characters you dislike. For example, there may be a piece of literature you have not enjoyed reading.

Reflection is about discovering who you are. You have already begun that journey with the I am journal activity. The start of a continuos reflective cycle.

Reflection is about continually examining your professional practice.

Reflection is about continually rewriting the movie, of which you are a part of. Each time there may be a different beginning, middle, and an ending. The point is no reflection will ever be the same, just like no movie is ever the same.

Reflection is about capturing others perspectives about your professional practice and listening to and reacting to other's feedback.

Reflection is messy, fun, and frustrating.

So, lights, camera, action! What are you waiting for?

Start writing your movie!

Barriers to Reflection

To this very day, I recall writing my first reflective account and being filled with dread. Dread that I was sharing myself with my tutor. It is worth noting and appreciating that reflection is not easy for everyone. There are several barriers to reflection, and if you face any of these, you should be open and honest and share your barriers with your tutor or mentor. You could face any of the following:

Fear

This is when you may be feeling you are not ready to reflect upon yourself and/or your professional practice. But believe me, we all must start somewhere, and you are best to submit a reflective account or have a reflective conversation so that you can receive feedback to positively impact the next part of your reflective journey. So, face the fear and reflect!

Exposure

Reflecting upon ourselves, our journey and expressing and sharing our emotions can leave us feeling exposed, and you may feel you are not ready for this. However, without sharing your feelings, emotions, and thoughts, I believe we cannot be truly reflective. Gibbs's (1998) model of reflection recognises emotions and how as part of our reflective practice it is important to reflect upon these. Be honest in recognising your emotions within your reflections and turn this barrier into a positive.

I can honestly say I have cried many times when I have spent hours planning a session, and it does not go according to plan. There is a lot to learn from exposing yourself to reflection. It will help you to recognise your emotions and reflect forward. Continuous reflection will support you to become more resilient and courageous. Appreciate that you are perfectly imperfect!

Demotivating

Reflection is wonderful when you have planned a session and everything has gone according to plan. However, if things go terribly wrong, then reflecting upon the experience may leave you feeling demotivated. But try to use this experience as a reflective learning process. Try to view the experience using others lens. Capturing others perspectives will support you in reflecting forward. In these moments, you could reflect using Brookfield's (1994) reflective theory. (You will cover Brookfield a little later in this chapter.)

Workload/Balance

As a student and/or practitioner, you can often be overwhelmed with work and/or essays. This can mean that reflections are pushed aside. However, as reflection is a journey, try to find a little time each day to reflect. This can be as simple as writing down a key word in your reflective journal at the end of each day to spending 20–30 minutes to bullet point or write a short reflective account. You could scribe 'what went well today' and/or 'what was a challenge today'. Keeping a log of continuous reflection will support you in future reflective accounts, all of which are useful to take along to appraisals of your progress. Capturing your reflections will also help you to write a developmental plan for your academic and professional journey.

Reflective Practice

Capturing the reflections of your lived experiences and emotions is part of the journey of self-discovery. It should be an enabling process which supports you in identifying and discovering your professional identity, values, and beliefs.

Reflective practice is when you apply your critical thinking to your experiences. Reflective practice is like opening a window on your professional practice and letting the sunshine flood in. When you open your reflective window practice and let the sunshine in, The sun will shine on the shiny moments of your professional practice.

However, we must also realise that sometimes when we open the window, it could let in the rain. This is when we need to appreciate that we may have to close the window for a while, change our practice, and reflect. This is when we must recognise that whilst reflective practice is personal, it is also influenced by a political, cultural, and societal context.

Let me explain.

Political Context

There is a wealth of legislation that governs and guides your work as an Early Years practitioner. For example, legislation concerned with equality, inclusion, and safeguarding. This legislation impacts upon your reflective practice and your role as an Early Years practitioner.

Cultural Context

We all have distinct cultural backgrounds. Every culture may differ in their values and beliefs, all of which will influence your reflective practice.

Societal Context

The society in which you live and work has an impact upon your reflective practice. Societies' socio-economic factors such as poverty and access to education, for example, will impact upon your reflective practice.

To summarise, reflective practice is when you set about to enquire about change. It should be self-affirming and empowering. Reflective practice is about being courageous and not choosing comfort over courage. (Brown 2018)

For example, consider how you may have heard, 'oh we have always done it this way' but upon reflection, you can see how something could be improved. This is when you need to step out of your comfort zone and be courageous. This is not easy as you begin your professional journey, but always remember that reflective practice is personal, and it is important to reflect upon why you are doing what you are doing?

Reflective practice is an opportunity for you to:

- be curious.
- identify your areas of development.
- identify your strengths.
- review your professional practice.
- share with others.
- receive feedback.
- use other's feedback to develop.
- increase self-awareness.
- apply critical and reflective theory.
- be emotive.

Reflective practice is muddy. For me, it is about being stuck in muddy moments and whilst you are stuck in the mud, staying there a while and reflecting in and on action. This relates to Schon's (1983) reflective theory which appears later in this chapter.

So, as you begin this reflective journey, I encourage you to:

- trust the process.
- trust and reflect upon your colleagues, peers and tutors feedback. seek out the positives in your reflections.
- give reflection dedicated time and energy.
- be respectful of other's perspectives.
- love your perfectly imperfect self.
- be ethical.

Reflective Activism

You may now be beginning to reflect, but you now need to act upon your reflections and be a reflective activist. Reflective activism is something I have developed over the years and has taken courage and confidence, and this may be the case for you too. However, reflective activism is our professional responsibility as Early Years practitioners.

As reflective activists, we must be advocates for our children and families: to hear and respond to the young child's voice, and to continually improve the quality of our provisions.

Do you consider yourself a reflective activist?

Here are some ways you can be a reflective activist.

Seek Change

Use your reflective activism to seek change that improves the enabling environment and ensures equality of opportunity or inclusion. These are just some examples of how you can use your reflections and your voice to seek change in a non-confrontational way who seek change and fulfil human needs. Use your voice to seek change in a non-confrontational way, for example to ensure equality of opportunity or inclusion for all.

Show Concern

Be the practitioner who is continuously reflecting and concerned about the education, health and care of all their children. Use your reflective activism to communicate your concerns and reflections with children, families, and colleagues.

Challenge Yourself

Use your reflective activism to try something new, to experiment, and to learn from success and failure.

Open Your Mind and Heart

A reflective activist will have their opinions but is also open to others perspectives. Use your reflective activism to approach your professional practice with an open mind and heart.

Communicate

A reflective activist enters relationships with others, communicating and listening. Use your reflective activism to engage in professional dialogue that seeks outstanding provision and accessibility for all.

In conclusion, use your reflective activism to be an agent of change. Create change, be the change. The work of Angie Hart (2013) leads us to reflect upon that being an agent of change may not be a smooth journey and we will face many obstacles.

Hart (2013) states that, as practitioners, we should maybe not just beat the odds but aim to change the odds.

Reflective Activism Journal Activity Part 1

Take some time to think about some of your professional practice from the previous week. Think of an incident, an activity, or a session where you feel you could have applied reflective activism.

Using the headings below, reflect and share some examples of where you used your reflective activism to seek change. How did you challenge yourself? How did you open your heart and mind and communicate?

Seek change.
Show concern.
Challenge yourself.
Open your mind and heart.
Communicate.

You can revisit this journal activity several times.

FIGURE 8.2   A tree outline

Reflective Activism Journal Activity Part 2. Copy the tree image into your journal.:

Leaves: Open your mind and heart and be honest. What challenges have you faced? You may need more than one leaf.

There may be more than one aspect of your professional practice you feel needs change. What change do you feel is needed?

Branches: What structures, practices, and/or policies exasperate the problems? What concerns you?

Trunk: What are the challenges you face in creating change? How can you overcome these? What support do you need? Who do you need to communicate with?

Roots: How as a reflective practitioner can you address the root of the problem? How can you create change?

Reflective Theory

In this section of the chapter, you will investigate a range of reflective theory and how you might apply these to your professional practice.

Each theorist is outlined in a worksheet, which you can copy and use to compliment your reflective journal entries and reflective writing.

Reflective Theory – Brookfield

Overview of Theory

Brookfield's reflective theory is a great starting point for your reflective journey and reflective writing. Brookfield (1994) suggests that when we reflect upon our professional practice, we should reflect using four lenses. These lenses are as follows:

Self-lens. This is often called your autobiographical lens. The self-lens according to Brookfield is the reflective account of your observations and feelings during a lived experience, your narrative.

Colleagues lens. This is your mentors, assessors, tutor, peers, and colleagues' lens. Often colleagues will offer you a different critical perspective that should enhance your autobiographical lens.

Children's lens. This is the child's lens, their thoughts, ideas, and reflections. These reflections can be challenging to capture. There are some ideas on how to capture a child's voice in the Research Practitioner chapter (Chapter 9).

Literature lens. This lens includes all the reading you may have done and also includes the legislation, frameworks, and policies you follow. Brookfield believes that as practitioners, we must use research and apply literature to our reflections to ensure that we develop a critically reflective lens.

Applying Theory to Professional Practice

Applying Brookfield's four lenses to your professional practice will guide you in your reflective activism. Applying all four lenses will give you a critical perspective on your professional practice. For example, when you receive feedback from your colleagues and/or your tutor, you can reflect and use their feedback to set areas of development and seek further opportunities to reflect and thrive.

Brookfield believes that reflective practitioners should not be prisoners of the past, meaning that you should seek change and not merely continue with the same-old because it has always been done this way. As a reflective practitioner, you should blow away apathy. Apathy is when someone, maybe a colleague, is demotivated and lack drives. Apathy does not bring change. Reflection and reflective practitioners do!

Summarise This Theory in Your Reflective Journal and Apply to Your Professional Practice

Summarise Brookfield's four reflective lenses.

Write a short extract of a session you were involved in last week.

Now reread your account and reflect upon how you could have captured the child's or your colleagues lens to support your reflective practice?

Finally, from the session you have reflected upon, what specific legislation (literature lens), do you feel informed your professional practice?

Reflective Theory – Schon

Overview of Theory

Schon's (1983) reflective theory suggests that as practitioners, we reflect **in and on action**. In its simplest form, this relates to your reflective thoughts **in action**. For example, these are the reflective thoughts you have when you are in the moment with children. Those thoughts you may have when you are up to your elbows in paint and your inner voice is telling you that maybe things are not going according to plan.

Reflecting on action are your reflections once an activity or a session is completed. This is the time when you can reflect upon the experience as a whole and possibly not only self-reflect but consider other's lens too (Brookfield).

Applying Theory to Professional Practice

Applying Schon's reflective theory is a little like wearing wellington boots. Let me explain. Schon talks about reflecting **in action** and **on action**. So, imagine being in your wellington boots in a field of mud with a group of children. It doesn't really matter what you are imagining the rest of the activity to be. The important bit is that you are there in the moment, in your wellington boots with the children and continually reflecting in action. These reflections may not be clear at the time as you are reflecting **in action** However, if you stay a while longer in the mud, maybe after the children have gone home, you will have chance to reflect **on action**.

Reflecting on action requires you to revisit those muddy moments. It requires you to relive the experience, digest it, and reflect. Schon believes that as practitioners, you should not view your reflective practice from the high ground. Meaning, you shouldn't merely stand above your professional practice but instead you should go to the lowlands, the swamp, or the mud and reflect.

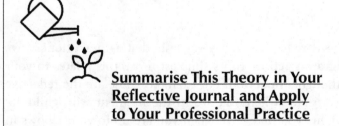

<u>Summarise This Theory in Your Reflective Journal and Apply to Your Professional Practice</u>

Summarise Schon's theory. Imagine you must explain Schon's theory to a peer. What would you say?

Now think of an experience from your professional practice. Pull on your wellington boots.

Explain how you reflected in action? What did you do in the moment to improve the experience?

Now reflect on action. Stay in the mud! What are your reflections? How would you change this experience if you were to revisit it?

Reflective Theory – Argyis and Schon

Overview of Theory

Argyis and Schon (1978) suggests reflection is divided into a single and double loop. A single loop represents reflection, with the double loop representing reflection and reflexivity. Reflexivity is the ability to examine your feelings and reactions, and this influences how you think or what you do.

In its simplest form, the single loop refers to the **What? So What? and What Now?** when reflecting upon an experience or a situation. Whereas the double loop question is **Why?**

Applying Theory to Professional Practice

Applying the single-loop questions – **What? So What? And What Now?** – is when as a practitioner you are reflecting upon an experience. This may be an activity that children are involved in such as play dough. It could be some children are not wishing to touch or feel the dough. As a reflective practitioner, you would be applying the single-loop questions: **What can I do? So, What next? What can I change? What can I do now?**

The double-loop question – **Why?** – is also something you will apply. You will reflect upon and ask yourself, **Why** did some children not interact? **Why** did I assume they all would? The **Why**, is where you can begin to reflect upon any assumptions you may have made prior to the activity.

Summarise This Theory in Your Reflective Journal and Apply to Your Professional Practice

Summarise Argyis and Schon's theory. Imagine you must explain this theory to a peer. What would you say?

Now reflect upon a recent experience. How did you apply the single-loop questions – **What can I do? So, What next? What can I change? What can I do now?**

How did you apply the double-loop question – **Why?**

What have you learnt from this experience?

Reflective Theory – Pendrey (2022)

Overview of Theory

My approach to reflection is represented by five Rs: **Recharge, Reimagine, Reflect, Revisit, and Real.** Due to the emotive nature of reflection, I believe you need time to **Recharge** immediately after an experience, especially if you have been observed. You need time to gather your thoughts. Shortly after this, you can begin to critically reflect and ask yourself questions such as, What would you do differently/What would I change? How? and Why? Which all encompass the R's, **Reimagine, Reflect and Revisit**.

The final R is for **Real**. I feel it is important that as you reflect, you keep it real. What I mean by this is to not write everything went smooth when it didn't. Be honest and share the disasters, the challenges, and possibly how low you felt in the moment.

This sense of reality is key in reflection. It is something to be celebrated. We might aim for perfection and outstanding practice, but does this happen every day of your professional practice?

Applying Theory to Professional Practice

Recharge, this can be anything from taking time after an observation to appreciate your emotions, to taking time to recharge and log your thoughts in your reflective diary. Secondly, you should **reimagine**. This is a continuous process. You should be time **reflecting** and reimagining the experience. Take time to note the positives and the negatives of the experience.

This will lead you to **revisit** the experience and consider the changes you may need to make to improve the experience and its outcomes. Even the most positive experiences can always be improved. Finally, be kind to yourself and be honest with yourself, your colleagues, and your tutor/mentor and **keep it real.** Reflect upon the experience openly and honestly.

Summarise This Theory in Your Reflective Journal and Apply to Your Professional Practice

Summarise the five Rs.

Journal a recent experience. Write this down or bullet point the main points of reflection from the experience.

Next, apply the five Rs. Add detail to each R. How can you use this approach to reflect in the future?

Reflective Theory – Gibbs

Overview of Theory

Possibly one of the most used reflective theories is Gibbs's (1998) reflective cycle. Gibbs's six stage cycle introduces you to the following stages, **description, feelings, evaluation, analysis, conclusion, and action plan**. You begin reflecting by describing the experience. Explore this in depth, do not assume the reader knows what you are saying, and **describe** each detail of the experience. Next, Gibbs's cycle requires you to reflect upon your **feelings**. Your feelings are very important. Once you are appreciated how you felt about the experience, you can then begin to **evaluate and analyse**.

As you begin to **analyse and evaluate**, apply your critical thinking. Evaluate the positives and negatives of the experience before analysing. Analysing is where you are trying to make sense of the experiences before finally concluding. **Concluding** requires you to create an action plan or reflect forward as to areas of improvement.

Applying Theory to Professional Practice

Gibbs's reflective theory is a continuous cycle. So, applying the reflective cycle is something you will do daily in your professional practice. Of course, every activity or session you are part of will not be captured in your reflective journal. However, whilst you might not be scribing the experience, you will be using your internal dialogue and this is still reflecting. Your inner voice will continually evaluate and analyse, and when the experience is over, you will most certainly reflect upon the experience and conclude. You will think to yourself what would I do next time I revisited this experience? What do I need to do to improve?

In your professional practice, it is important to share this continuous inner dialogue with your peers, colleagues, assessor, tutor, or mentor. They are there to support you and watch you thrive.

Summarise This Theory in Your Reflective Journal and Apply to Your Professional Practice

Summarise Gibbs's theory. Imagine you must explain Gibbstheory to a peer. What would you say?

Draw Gibbs's reflective cycle in your journal.

Now think of an experience from your professional practice. Try to break down the experience and relate to each area of Gibbs's cycle?

Create an action plan and share this with your mentor and/ or tutor.

Having covered a range of reflective theory and models, you should now read the following reflective account. After reading the account, take time to apply some of the reflective theory and models to the account. This will support you as you move forward in reflecting upon your own experiences.

Reflective Account – Storytelling Experience

Read the following reflective account by Tara. Take some time to reflect and answer the reflective questions.

Tara Copard is the creator of Chameleon and a Family Support Worker.

Celebration Day at school is a big deal, it's an annual fun-filled event day at the end of Spring term for children's wellbeing to mark gaining our Thrive School of Excellence Award. This year included 'Hello Yellow' to raise money for a mental health charity. I had planned to go round each KS1 class storytelling. Last year, I read from my favourite books and initially intended to do the same this year. However, in a moment of madness, I decided to tell a story I had written myself using prompt cards and props. As the time grew nearer, I became more and more apprehensive and nervous, frequently asking myself what possessed me to even think this was a good idea?

As the day drew closer, I was wobbling, wondering if I should just play it safe and read other's stories. I pushed through the worry and began my storytelling journey in the first Reception class. I was blown away, I had their attention, they were interacting with me, and it was such a buzz, more than I had hoped for. As I travelled through the classrooms, I became more confident, more animated, and really enjoyed myself, especially as it was all my own work coming to life and being received so well by those whose opinions can be tough and let's face it, brutally honest.

Although it was an amazing experience, on reflection, I feel it can be improved on. The experience would have worked better if I had memorised the story as there were there were pauses when I needed to put my prompt cards down to use the props. Next time, I may ask for some child volunteers to help me with the characters so that I can move freely around the room among the children instead of sitting in one spot.

I intended this story to be in book form, which would still be great, but making it more interactive and visual worked better than I could have imagined.

FIGURE 8.3 A set of Chameleons ready for story time with young children

 **Reflective Questions**

Which reflective theories do you feel apply to Tara's reflection account, her actions, and her emotions? And why?

What key messages have you taken away from this account?

Reflective Writing

Now you have begun your reflective journey and examined reflective theory and models, you are now ready to write reflectively. This is whereas an experienced practitioner, I always refer to my reflective journal. My journal contains words, images, and reflections of things I have sometimes forgotten.

Reflective writing can be challenging, but let me refer you back to that bowl of spaghetti with its entanglements and twists of pasta interlocked into one another. Beginning to write reflectively requires you to detangle your reflections, extract elements of your lived experiences, reflect upon your values and beliefs, reflect upon your reflective activism, and then put all this into words, a reflective account.

You may be asked to reflect upon a critical incident or produce a reflective account. A critical incident is an event, experience, or a process that requires a response. The response being a reflection and a course of action for improvement. A reflective account is more of a description of an event or experience which requires reflection. You could argue there seems to be little difference and maybe there isn't, but it is always wise to be aware of the language used within your course and check with your tutor exactly what is required.

However, a reflective account or a critical incident both require you to plan, craft, and write your critical reflections.

The first thing to consider is that when you begin to write reflectively, you will find it emotive and possibly even frustrating. You may feel:

- Angry
- Scared
- Exposed
- Freedom
- Autonomy
- Perplexed
- Enlightened
- Empowered
- Motivated
- Deflated or
- Encouraged

Use these emotions within your reflective account. Be honest and open. Discuss and reflect upon how you may have felt perplexed with an activity, a session, or a professional discussion. Equally, celebrate the positive emotions you may have felt. Critically reflect upon how you use the experience, the critical incident to reflect forward and realign emotions.

Let's go back to a reference I made earlier about shining a light on your professional practice. Think of this as you begin to plan your writing. Also, refer to your reflective journal. You will be amazed at some of the minor details of an experience you may have forgotten but is logged in your journal.

Reflective writing is personal and an exploration of your experiences, feelings, thoughts, and emotions. It requires honesty, transparency and if you recall realism. Try not to be too subjective and approach your writing willing to accept others 'perspectives.

Make a Plan

Take time to plan and gather notes, reflections, and key words from your journal. Read through these and consider what reflective theory aligns to your reflections. Have a clear focus.

Read

Take time to read and research any literature that will support your work. Note the citations.

Remember

Remember your reflective writing is more than a step by step description account of an experience. You need to apply your critical thinking and critically analyse your reflections.

Thriving

Critically Analyse

Question what you have written, apply your critical thinking, and begin to analyse the experience in more depth.

Ask Questions

As you begin to write ask yourself the questions, **what, why, how,** and so, **what?** Then go back and revisit your answers in more depth. **Have you been critically reflective?**

Identify

Identify your areas of development and your strengths. Reflect upon both.

Don't Forget You!

Put yourself in the spotlight. Do not assume as a reader, we can see or feel the experience. Share and reflect upon your values, beliefs, professional identity, and emotions with the reader.

Conclude

Conclude your account with some of your reflective activism. Share with the reader the impact this experience has had upon you as a practitioner.

End with a conclusion.

- What is the focus?
- What happened?
- Reimagine the experience. Write down your thoughts, ideas, and feelings about the experience?

- Consider others lens and perspectives.
- Include any feedback from children or your tutor.
- Apply reflective theory.
- Use I.
- Reflect forward – what would you do next time and why?
- Proofread.
- Edit.
- Review.
- Check spellings, and grammar.
- Does your reflective account flow?
- Get someone else to read your work – be brave!
- Make your final amendments.
- Congratulate yourself on your submission.

Planting your seeds of knowledge and understanding

At the end of this chapter, you are now ready to plant the seeds of knowledge you have discovered about reflection, reflective activism, and reflective theory.

You are now ready to reflect upon your understanding of how you will be a reflective practitioner in your professional practice.

Take a moment to look back at the topics, and using the image, reflect upon:

What is reflection and reflective practice?

What is reflective activism?

Which reflective theories do you relate to and why?

Why is it important to be a reflective practitioner?

What do you think the reflective thoughts are of the practitioner observing these two children sitting in a cardboard box?

FIGURE 8.4 Two young children sitting in a cardboard box

9 The Research Practitioner

In this chapter, you will be introduced to what is research and how research informs your professional practice. You will have the opportunity to reflect upon the importance of research and how you can capture the child's voice within your research.

The seeds of knowledge explored within the chapter are as follows:

What is research?
Research practitioner qualities
How does research inform you?
Research terminology
Types of research
The Research roadmap
Research tips
Research and children's voices

DOI: 10.4324/9781003361442-12

What Is Research?

The word research can often seem onerous, and you might even feel you are not ready to conduct research. However, you are a researcher every single day of your professional practice. For example, consider the adaptions you may have made during an activity with a child, this is research.

Consider the conversations you may have had with a child's parent, this is research. Not all research has to be formal. Not all research has to lead you to a dissertation. Research is being curious, reflecting and investigating facts, sources, or materials to seek improvement and reach new conclusions.

Research is an investigation, a study of an issue or a topic that sparks your curiosity. Research seeks to identify any gaps in existing knowledge, for example any gaps in Early Years education. Identifying these gaps and commencing your research should aim to not only expand your own knowledge and understanding of the subject but also generate new ideas, concepts, or approaches for your professional practice. This occurs when the research practitioner approaches and conducts research systematically.

Finally, research is essential in helping us as practitioners to advance knowledge, to seek change, to inform our professional practice, to inform policies, and to be innovative and up to date.

Research Practitioner Qualities

A research practitioner is a practitioner who utilises their curiosity and acts upon their reflections to create change. A research practitioner is an agent of change, a practitioner who is both reflective and curious about their professional practice.

These qualities are categorised under the following headings:

1. **Personal effectiveness**
2. **Cognitive skills**
3. **Dissemination and engagement**

Personal Effectiveness

Patience

You already have this quality as you have entered the world of Early Years, and as practitioners, we have an abundance of patience. However, this is a quality you will also need as you commence and undertake research. Research is a marathon and not a sprint, a saying you may have already heard. Research takes time, and if you are just setting out on your research journey, you will need patience. For example, you may have a research idea/proposal that is rejected and requires you to rethink your topic. You need to be patient and work with your tutors to rework a research proposal.

You will need patience as you begin reading and searching for literature to support your research. You also need patience as you analyse data and when you write up your findings for your research project. So, start to reframe your thinking towards research. Be aware that research takes time, effort, determination, and patience.

Enthusiasm

Entering research with enthusiasm is essential. You should choose a research topic that ignites a spark of enquiry within. You should excited to begin the research process when you have chosen a topic that you are enthusiastic about. However, I am aware that research can be challenging, and you may feel overwhelmed or a little disengaged at times. This could lead to you pushing your research aside. For example, you may concentrate on other things and start procrastinating. This is when that little voice in your head pops up and says, 'I just need to do this first before I start my research'.

However, research should be a continuous cycle of inquiry and so you should organise your research, and take time to work on your research regularly.

Thriving

Commitment

This quality is closely linked with patience. A research practitioner must show commitment, commitment to commence and complete their research. In addition to this, a research practitioner is committed to quality and improvement, the very reason you research.

During your research, you will be communicating with your peers, your team, your research supervisor, tutor, and participants. Whichever form of communication you use, ensure it is ethical.

Cognitive Skills

Knowledge and Understanding

A research practitioner needs to have a deeper knowledge and understanding of their subject matter. For you, this is Early Years education, the theories, philosophers, concepts and approaches to play, learning, and child development and more.

A research practitioner keeps abreast of new initiatives and changes by reading, collaborating, and networking to enhance their knowledge and understanding.

You will need to source, read, and critically analyse text to support your knowledge and understanding of your research area.

ICT – Information and Communications Technology

We live in a digital world where all books, journals, legislation, and frameworks are stored online. You need to be proficient in these areas to locate resources for your research. You need to source reading material/research that is valid and reliable. You may have access to an online library as a student and use this facility to support you in your research. Search for books and academic journals accurately and if you find this a challenge, use the most excellent resource of all, the librarian!

Critical Thinking

A research practitioner is a critical thinker. Critical thinking is the cognitive process of analysing, evaluating information, and reflection. Analysing is where you use your critical thinking to segment, examine, and critique information, for example the positives and negatives of a piece of literature. Analysing is also when you can apply your critical thinking to identify key information or facts that are poignant for your research.

Using your critical thinking to evaluate will help you to the strengths and weaknesses of an argument. Evaluating is also essential in determining what is relevant information for your research and to seek alternative perspectives to support your viewpoint, your argument, and your research.

Moreover, applying critical thinking to your role as a researcher will help you to be reflective about your own bias and assumptions.

Dissemination and Engagement

Communication

Communication is a quality a research practitioner needs throughout all the stages of research. A research practitioner needs to first communicate their proposal/idea and continue communicating until their research is complete. Upon completion of any research, a research practitioner needs to communicate and share their findings with others, disseminating their results and the impact of their research to a wider audience. This audience could be as intimate as your work colleagues or a national conference.

Ethical

Every research practitioner needs to be ethical. Ethical means that you must follow ethical guidelines set out by your organisation and BERA. BERA stands for the British Education Research Association. BERA is the leading authority for research in education in the UK.

As a research practitioner, you must follow ethical guidelines such as those outlined by BERA (2018).

These ethical guidelines highlight your responsibilities to the participants in your research. For example, BERA guidelines outline how you must gain informed consent from your research participants and ensure that no participant faces harm from involvement in the research. BERA will also guide you on how to store data and ensure privacy.

In addition to BERA guidelines, you also need to be aware of the General Data Protection Act (2018). The General Data Protection Act (2018) has strict data protection principles that you need to follow to ensure that all data collected is used lawfully, fairly, and transparently.

This might seem a little daunting at this stage in your career, but it is essential that the research practitioner is ethical.

 **Journal Activity – Qualities**

Take time to look back at the qualities needed to be a research practitioner.

Use your journal to reflect upon which qualities you feel you may need to develop to become a research practitioner?

What support do you need? Next, take time to complete the following basic self-analysis of your research qualities and effectiveness. This will support you in identifying areas in which you may need to develop and the support you may need.

Using each category, score yourself from 1 to 10.

A score of 1–5 means you have identified this as an area of development and will need support.

A score of 5–8 means you are quite confident in this area but
  may need some support.

A score of 9–10 means you are confident in this area and need
  little or no support.

Once you have completed this activity, share the results with
your research supervisor, tutor, or research colleagues/peers.

Personal Effectiveness	Score 1–10	What Support Do You Need?
Patience		
Enthusiasm		
Commitment		
Cognitive Skills		
Knowledge and understanding		
Information and Communications Technology (ICT)		
Critical thinking		
Dissemination and Engagement		
Communication		
Ethics		

Developing all these qualities takes time. However, as a research
practitioner, the more you reflect upon these qualities and the more
you research, you will develop a tool kit of research skills. A research
practitioner must have the knowledge and understanding of ethics,
research methodology, research methods, data collection, analysis,

and interpretation. A research practitioner will then be able to enter the word of Early Years, designing research projects, undertake research, and use their research findings to enhance and impact upon the Early Years sector.

How Does Research Inform You?

Research is essential in informing your professional practice. It expands your knowledge and understanding of the sector and supports your journey from being to thriving.

By staying informed about Early Years education, you will be able to apply new knowledge, concepts, and theory into your professional practice. However, always be prepared to challenge research, this is one of the qualities of a research practitioner. Don't be afraid to apply critical thinking and challenge research, questioning how you are informed by the research and how you feel you would apply this research to your practice?

As practitioners, we are informed by other professionals and experts who have all at some point used research to inform their decision making and advance knowledge.

Research aims to identify gaps and address problems and challenges within the Early Years sector, the wider community and society.

Research informs us. Being informed ensures that as practitioners, you play a vital role in shaping the future of Early Years education.

Research Terminology

As a research practitioner, at the start of your research journey, it is important to be aware of the types of research you may undertake. You may need to read up further and discuss your research methods with your tutor, research supervisor, or your workplace/placement so that your research methods are aligned to the research topic as well as being ethical. The terminology of research can also be confusing, so let's begin with a definition of research words to support you.

Methodology

Methodology is a systematic approach to your research. The specific methodology you choose for your research depends upon the aim and objectives of your research.

Methods

Methods are the techniques you use within your research, for example surveys, questionnaires, and interviews. The methods you choose must align to your methodology.

Triangulation

Triangulation in research is an approach that involves using various methods, sources or perspectives to enhance the validity and credibility of your research.

Literature Review

A literature review is a systematic review of resources such as books, journals, reports, and other literature. It involves identifying, analysing, and evaluating key points within the literature.

Ethics

Ethics involves protecting the welfare and the rights of all participants within your research. As a researcher, you must follow an ethical code of conduct.

Data Analysis

Data analysis is the process of inspecting, dissecting, and interpreting your data. It is the process of extracting key themes, experiences, and insights. It involves drawing conclusions and making future recommendations based the data collected and analysed.

Dissemination

Dissemination means sharing. It refers to how you will disseminate/ share the results and recommendations from your research with a wider audience.

Validity

Validity derives from the Latin word meaning strong. In your research, validity is crucial. It refers to how accurately your research methods measure what you intend to measure.

Reliability

Reliability in research refers to the stability and consistency of the research measures, You need to ensure that the research measures are dependable, consistent and reliable.

Analysis

Analysis means examining and interpreting data collected from your research methods.

Types of Research

There are different types of research as follows.

Qualitative Research

Qualitative research aims to interpret people's perspectives and experiences. Qualitative research involves research methods such as observations and interviews.

Quantitative Research

Quantitative research is a more systematic approach. It involves the collection of numerical data through surveys and experiments.

Mixed Method Research

Mixed methods research is a combination of quantitative and qualitative approaches. You can use both these approaches in a single research project. This involves combining the collection of numerical data (quantitative) with other non-numerical data (qualitative).

Research Roadmap

As a research practitioner, you should consider your research design a little like a roadmap where you must follow directions to ensure you reach your destination. Imagine designing research, if you will, a little like entering a postcode on a sat nav. You pop in your final destination, but before you can set off and reach the final destination, you have to turn a few corners and travel down a few different streets before the sat nav announces, 'you have reached your final destination'.

To support you in your research design, here is a template that you might find useful, here is a template that will support you in your research design. You can use this to help you plan the start of your journey as a research practitioner.

Use the template to write down your research ideas. Share your ideas with your tutor, research supervisor, or team.

Use your network of support to ensure that the research you wish to undertake is ethical, valid, and reliable.

Name of Researcher	
Research Supervisors Name	
Research Title	

Research Question/s	
Literature Review	
Research Methodology	
Research Method/Data Collection	
Data Analysis	
Research Findings	

Research Tips

Using your research template, you can now begin to undertake your research.

Here are a few tips for you as you begin your research.

Be Organised

Begin your research by organising your resources. Start with a research diary, this is a place where you can capture your ideas, research questions, log meetings, and set goals. Research is also reflective, so capture your reflections.

Keep meticulous notes. For example, as you read, organise your citations; there is nothing worse than losing a quote that fits so well in your work. Believe me when I say I have done this in my own work, so it is advice that comes from the heart!

As you research, you will find your own way of organising your notes, but being organised is essential in managing your research effectively.

Plan Your Research Design

Using the research template as a guide, you can now begin to carefully design your methodology, methods of data collection, analysis, and ethical approval.

Define Your Research Topic and Questions

Spend some time thinking about your research topic.
What are the aims and objectives of the research?
What are the research questions?
What do you want to achieve?

Bucknall (2012) suggests that as researchers, we view research questions as 'big' and 'little' questions. This is a useful way to approach your research. You could consider the 'big' question to be the aim of your research, leading you to explore what the 'little' questions? What are you aiming to discover from undertaking your research?

In addition, you should plan time to spend with your tutor, your team or colleagues agreeing on the validity of the research and its possible impact.

Triangulation

As you begin the research process, reflect upon how you might apply triangulation to your research.

Triangulation can be applied to your research by the following:

Methods triangulation is using multiple methods to research your topic.
Data triangulation is collecting data using different methods. For example, gathering data through interviews and observations is triangulation.
Theory triangulation is using different theories or hypothesis to investigate your topic.

Begin a Literature Review

A literature review is where you will begin to utilise your research qualities and begin to search for existing knowledge around the topic of your research. You will also research and try to identify any gaps in the literature available. It is in this part of the process that as a research practitioner, you are trying to demonstrate why your research is worthy of investigation. You will be aiming to show your tutor, colleagues, or institution how your research will add value to an existing body of knowledge and evidence relating to Early Years.

This part of the research requires patience and time to research, to source books, and/or journals relating to your research area.

Ethical Approval

Ensure you adhere to ethical guidelines when conducting your research. As a research practitioner, you have a duty of care towards your research participants. All participants must consent to their involvement in your research. You must ensure all the participants in your research are protected from harm and that they can withdraw from your research without consequences. As a research practitioner, it is crucial that you uphold all ethics so that you maintain your professional integrity and your research is credible.

Collecting Data

Having planned your research and gained ethical approval, you will begin to collect and then analyse data. You need to be clear that the methods you use for collecting data are appropriate for the type of research you are undertaking.

You then need to plan your data collection methods, for example planning your questionnaires, surveys, observation schedule or interview questions, if these are the methods you have chosen. Seek guidance in this process; you need to make sure that the questions you are asking, for example, are not misleading and will give you the information you need. You may also wish to do a pilot sample as this is useful as part of gaining feedback regarding the design of your questions/questionnaire.

As you begin this process, use your research diary to capture your notes and reflections. Your research diary can be a useful tool to take along to your supervisor meetings.

When you have designed your data collection methods, you must follow ethical guidelines on data protection. How will you be ensuring that each participants data is protected? Will you be giving each participant a pseudonym? A pseudonym is when you use a fictious name to replace the participant's real name. For example, Banksy, this is a pseudonym for an artist whose real name no one knows! A pseudonym could also be a number, a letter, or anything that does not reveal the identity of the participant.

Having done all of this, then comes the exciting bit, collecting the data. Here, you will need a research schedule. When and where you will be conducting the research?

Analysing Data

Once all the data is collected, you need to organise and analyse the data. This can be overwhelming, and this is why you need to be organised. Plan your time and analyse methodically and systematically in line with your research methodology.

Analysing data can adopt several approaches. For example, if you are conducting a qualitative piece of research, you might use thematic analysis. Thematic analysis looks for themes or patterns within the data. The emerging themes will inform your future recommendations.

Alternatively, you might use content analysis. Content analysis can include counting the frequency of words, which can then provide with a percentage. This is more quantitative as opposed to using the data to identify and analyse themes and interpreting the data more qualitatively. You can use this information as a starting point to research further how best to analyse the data in your research project

Presenting Your Findings

Presenting, sharing, and disseminating are all words you may encounter as part of your research journey. All these words are essentially asking you the same thing. How will you distribute the findings of your research? How will you share your knowledge with others? For example, will you be writing a report? Will you be presenting at a team meeting or a conference? How will you share the impact of the research with others? Who will you be sharing the research findings with?

Networking and collaborating with others in your field will give you the opportunity to share your research findings. It will also give you a platform from which to share the recommendations from the research. It will give you the chance to share your reflective, research journey.

Research and Children's Voices

As you gain confidence as a research practitioner, you can begin to consider how you will include children's voices within your research. Capturing the child's voice will give you an insight and a different perspective into their needs, likes, dislikes, development, and learning.

There are some further considerations for you to consider when researching with children.

These include the following

Ethics

You must always gain consent from all participants in your research. However, if your research involves children, you will need to consider how you will gain their consent via their parents/carers. Using the research template, you will need to carefully consider which methodology and methods suit your research. Whichever methodology and methods you adopt will need to be developmentally and age appropriate.

Once consent is gained, you will also need to ensure that all children are granted privacy and all data collected is stored securely.

And don't forget any participant within your research always has the right to withdraw.

Communication

You need to consider how you adapt your communication and language to suit the age and stage of development of the children within your research. Take time to consider the use of verbal and non-verbal communication and visual aids and how this may be used to capture data.

Age and Stage Appropriate Methods

Depending upon the age and developmental stage of the child, you will need to take time to consider how you will capture data. Some methods may include observations, art based, or creative ways methods or focus groups. Clarke and Moss (2011) developed something called the MOSAIC approach. You may wish to research this approach further. A simple definition is for you to picture a mosaic. And imagine how each mosaic is made up of lots of different tiles, then consider how each tile is a component of your research. Each tile is a tool and a method of capturing the child's voice. These tools might be observations, stories, photographs, or objects, all of which are used to capture the child's voice and perspectives.

Using this approach will develop children as researchers. This approach will develop children's confidence, autonomy, and give children a voice within your research.

Thriving

Finally, whatever methods you choose, they need to be child-centred and so take time to reflect how children can be active participants within your research. You need to ensure that the child's voice is captured and heard. Involvement in the research needs to make the child feel empowered, give them autonomy, and not be a tokenistic level of involvement.

Research Environment

All research environments should be safe spaces. A space of ease where all participants, especially children, feel safe, secure, and comfortable to express their views and opinions. Children should feel they have autonomy and freedom of speech.

Consider how as a research practitioner, you build a rapport with your research participants, particularly children. The relationship between researcher and participants is essential in gathering data that is reliable and valid. Reflect upon your positionality within the research. Positionality is when as a researcher you reflect upon your own values, beliefs, and experiences and how these personal perspectives may influence how you conduct the research and interpret the data.

Analyse, Feedback, and Disseminate

Analysing children's data can include thematic analysis or content analysis which you have already been introduced to within this chapter. Researching with children requires you to reflect upon how you will share the outcomes of the data analysis with them? How will you feedback your research findings with the children? You will need to consider your communication style. You need to reflect upon any necessary adaptations and reasonable adjustments that are required in order for the child's voice should be heard at every stage of the research!

Planting Your Seeds of Knowledge and Understanding

At the end of this chapter, you are now ready to plant the seeds of knowledge you have discovered about research.

You are now ready to reflect upon your understanding of how you will be a research practitioner in your professional practice.

Take a moment to look back at the topics, and using the image, reflect upon:

What is research?

What research qualities do you need to develop?

Why do you need these qualities?

Why do practitioners need to continually research?

The practitioners in the image are researching curriculum. Why is this important? How will this type of research impact upon their professional practice? How will this research impact upon the children and parents within their setting?

FIGURE 9.1   Two practitioners researching

10 The Developing Practitioner

As you begin to interact with the final chapter of this book, you are now possibly on your way to being fully qualified or researching why professional development is important in readiness for your new role in Early Years.

In this chapter, you are invited to consider what is professional development and why engaging with professional development opportunities is important in your role as an Early Years practitioner. Moreover, you will explore several ways to engage in professional development and consider how you will capture your knowledge, understanding, and reflections as you develop and thrive.

The seeds of knowledge explored within the chapter are as follows:

Professional development
The benefits of professional development
Reflecting and capturing your professional development
Your gifts and experiences
Professional development experiences

DOI: 10.4324/9781003361442-13

Professional Development

Professional development is a term I recall this term from way back in my Nursery Nurse days. My memory of this term is a negative one and tinged with some sadness and despair. The reason for this is because in my Nursery Nursing days and within several institutions I worked, I was not invited to any professional development. Instead of joining the teaching staff in professional development opportunities, I was often given the task of laminating, creating displays, or tidying up.

These were the moments I call my 'Cinderella moments' because just like Cinderella, I can honestly say, I was never invited to the ball or indeed invited to any training that would develop my skills and knowledge. My professional development came from my own interactions with literature and the 'hands on' part of my role as an NNEB.

Today, professional development, also referred to as CPD, continuous professional development, is something I hope is much more inclusive, developmental, and personalised for all educators and students. Whatever the term, professional development or CPD, I urge you to take part in as much as you can to develop your knowledge, to impart your own knowledge and ideas with others, and to make connections.

There are several ways in which to partake in professional development which we will also explore in this final chapter. However, let's begin with why engaging with professional development will support your being, belonging, and thriving as an Early Years practitioner.

The Benefits of Professional Development

Professional development is important for several reasons. These include These include:

Enhancing Your Professional Knowledge and Skills

Once you are qualified and employed, you will need to continue to enhance your professional skills and knowledge. You can do this independently by reading, researching, and attending events or by taking part in mandatory training as part of your job. A mixture of both will enhance the knowledge and skills you have already gained from your studies and vocational training. Take advantage of enhancing your knowledge and skills by listening to your colleagues, parents, and networking with the wider community of practice. All of these will inform your professional practice. It is also worth journaling any new knowledge and skills so that you can reflect upon your current practice. You can revisit your journal, refresh your memory as to what was covered within your training, and later add the impact this has had upon you as a practitioner.

Enhancing the Outcomes for Your Organisation/Workplace

Your organisation/workplace will also have targeted areas of improvement which you may be asked to develop as part of your role. These areas of improvement may be due to feedback from an inspection or part of a new initiative for your organisation. All improvements will not only enhance the outcomes for your organisation but also enhance your professional skills and knowledge. Collectively, you are working together to improve the outcomes for children and families.

Keeping Up to Date with New Initiatives

In an ever-changing world, it is important to keep up with new initiatives. These initiatives can range from changes in curriculum to the introduction of new technology. As professionals, we are informed by several sources, media, innovations, experts, advocates, and research, all of which may introduce you to a new way of thinking, or approach to your professional practice. This is where you need to recall the importance of being curious. Being curious about new initiatives will improve your professional practice and has the potential to advance your career.

Personal Growth

Undertaking professional development will increase your confidence, advance your knowledge, and give you the opportunity to reflect upon your reason for being an Early Years practitioner. Gaining new skills and knowledge is empowering. Professional development can ignite a spark within you and support you to reflect upon how you might progress in your career.

Networking

You can network in so many ways. Social media is a great way to network and connect with others. You can follow fellow Early Years professionals, groups, blogs, magazines, and academic journals and interact with posts to gain new knowledge and skills. You should explore all opportunities to connect with your communities of practice in your local are. This is a great way to begin to engage in professional dialogue with other professionals, to have reflective conversation and share ideas.

 ### <u>Reflective Account – Curiosity Is a Spark</u>

The following reflective account is from Tina, an Early Years Foundation Stage Lead. She talks about a recent professional development session and curiosity.

Read the following account. Then, stop, reflect, and answer the reflective questions.

Curiosity is the 'spark' that ignites desire to explore a thought, idea, and action. How does the spark begin? It can be the tiniest provocation, an object, a story, or an experience.

I recently attended a CPD training event that suggested to create a spark the provocation needs to be explicit to encourage curiosity. I have pondered and reflected upon this suggestion; initially, I considered how I encourage children's curiosity in practice. My reception class planning is explicit, comprised of clearly structured focus activities which is necessary to provide the framework for development and assessment. In addition to this, the continuous provision is explicit and purposeful.

During my reflection, I asked myself how we encourage the children's curiosity?

As an Early Years team, we spend time reflecting on the spaces; these need to be purposeful, calm, and offer a range of resources and experiences that are accessible to the children. I have observed the children's curiosity is evident when they are enabled to follow their own interests and skills, they enjoy. For example, a child in my setting loves mark making and role play; he enjoys being a police officer who looks out for any wrong doings and ensures these are dealt with accordingly. I frequently observe this child's play following the direction of the child's mark making messages.

As an Early Years team, we observe listen, and develop all child's play and curiosity. Ait is important to offer each child a skilfully posed a thought or an idea that could develop ignite a spark for the child to extend his interest to the next level.

It is also important that Early Years staff have a deep understanding of development and know the children well. The key to igniting the spark is observing, what makes individual child 'tick'; the first step to curiosity provocation is engagement in purposeful activity.

My reflective practice is a daily reminder of the importance of explicit, purposeful, and exciting curriculum planning that will become the platform to ignite children's curiosity. Engaging the children in exciting experiences is the centre of igniting the spark, and with time, space, and skilled adults, the spark may evolve to a magnitude of exploration, joy, and learning.

Returning to the CPD event I attended, I took away one word, 'explicit'. Explicit can and should remain in our thoughts and become the nucleus of our own professional curiosity. In the weeks that followed the CPD event, I continually observed and reflected upon our Early Years provision; the spaces, the resources and learning experiences.

 **Reflective Questions**

Summarise the key messages from Tina's CPD session

What was the specific impact of the session upon her and her team?

What do you feel was the impact of the CPD upon the children in the setting?

Can you think of a recent professional development training event you have been part of?

Did you take time to reflect upon the impact of the session?

I wish to end this reflective account with a reflection of my own. I want to share with you that not all training you attend will be relevant to your role, and it may not even be engaging. However, I believe you can take away something from all professional development sessions, even if that is you saying to yourself, 'I won't be doing things that way, but thank you for the session'.

Reflecting and Capturing Your Professional Development

Reflecting upon your professional development is important. It is part of being a curious and reflective practitioner. Taking time to reflect upon the process of professional development will give you the opportunity to consider how you can apply what you have learnt to your professional practice. You may also reflect and identify gaps in your knowledge and consider how to address these gaps.

There are several ways to take part in professional development. Professional development does not have to be course or a training session; it can be a piece of reading, a blog, or networking with others on social media. All of these are professional development. There are also some institutions that offer free training, free membership, and access to resources.

After any professional development activity, it is important to pause and reflect upon what you have taken away from the session. What were the key messages? For example, did the session impact upon your thinking and how might it influence your professional practice? This is a perfect opportunity to journal and capture your reflections.

Use your journal to scribe your reflections, the impact of the professional development activity, and any areas of development you have identified. You could also journal an action plan of how you will implement what you have learnt. You could also journal how you will cascade your new information, skills, and knowledge with others.

Your Gifts and Experiences

As your journal your professional development, you might wish to stop a while and consider your gifts and experiences.

What are gifts and experiences?

So, here is my thinking. I believe as Early Years practitioners, we have our own unique set of gifts. These gifts are what we bring along with us every day into our professional practice. For example, some of my gifts are creativity, divergent thinking, and organisation. I use all my gifts on a day-to-day basis in my personal and professional life.

My gift of creativity is important to me, and I am not creative in that I can paint and draw masterpieces, but I am creative in my pedagogical approaches. For example, I often teach with no power point and if you have ever been taught by me, you will know I have had you singing, learning rhymes linked to theoretical concepts, and encouraged you to use objects for discussions and debates. This also links to my gift of divergent thinking. I don't just think outside the box; I think in, out, and around it! What I mean by this is that I am happy to sit a while and think of different ways to approach an activity and a problem, and often I do come up with some off-the-wall ideas. However, I am quite happy and brave enough to share my divergent thinking with others.

My other gifts of organisation and reflection have served me well in my career. I am sometimes too organised, and yes, I am that person with post it notes and a pen on my bedside table! And of course, I am a reflective practitioner. I am always reflecting and seeking new experiences and approaches to teaching and learning.

However, whilst we all have gifts, and you might wish to take time now to consider what are your gifts, we also need a variety of rich and engaging experiences that will enhance our gifts or even maybe lead us to discover new ones. Your daily professional practice and the experiences of professional development will all increase your skills and knowledge as you thrive as an early years practitioner.

Professional Development Experiences

There are several ways to engage with professional development. These include:

Online Learning

Online learning can be as simple as your engagement with social media platforms such as X, LinkedIn, or Facebook. You can follow and interact with Early Years authors, groups, and individuals who all openly share their work. You can join in chats and forums. You can ask questions within groups or to individuals who will be more than happy to support your professional development. Choose your choice of followers and always practice safe internet use. Don't fall into the trap of buying into anything or giving away your details. You are only here to exchange knowledge.

Research and Publications

There are many individuals in the field of Early Years who have written publications. These publications can be books, blogs, or academic journals. Any interaction with any of these is professional development and will support your thriving journey. You can read something that really resonates with you, and you can also read something which you can critique. This is an important aspect of reading. This is building upon your critical thinking, critical analysis, and critical reflection.

When I read, I only ever set out to read a few pages at a time. I read then I stop! I sit and reflect upon the reading. I highlight key words and then I journal my thoughts. You might read and reflect very differently to me, but the message is, reading is professional development.

Visits and Networking

Visiting other settings is an amazing experience. You can always pick up a new idea, concept, or approach to enhance your professional practice. Every setting is unique and whilst you may have finished your training, you should continue to network with others. This will widen your community of practice and provide you with free professional development.

Professional Associations

There are several professional Early Years associations. These often require you to be a member, and there may be a fee for joining. However, they do offer you opportunity to connect with like-minded people and the association will offer you a wealth of resources. For example, you may have access to a regular newsletter, online training, or even an academic journal. Each professional association differs, but all offer you the opportunity for professional development.

Mentor or Coach

In your workplace, you may be offered a mentor or a coach. A mentor is someone who may have more experience than yourself. A mentor is someone who will use their gifts and experiences to offer you guidance and support. A coach is a little different to a mentor. A coach will form a collaborative relationship with you and support you in setting to achieve your professional development goals. Both roles will support you in unlocking your gifts and to reach your full potential.

Workshops

Workshops are usually short sessions with a subject focus. These can be both paid and free events.

Conferences

Conferences can be held over one or more days and include keynote speakers and workshop sessions, where you can work in groups, debate, discuss, and reflect upon a subject.

 Planting your seeds of knowledge and understanding

At the end of this chapter, you are now ready to plant the seeds of knowledge you have discovered about professional development.

You are now ready to reflect upon your understanding of how you will be a developing practitioner in your professional practice.

Take a moment to look back at the topics, and using the image, reflect upon:

What is professional development?

What are the benefits of professional development?

What are your gifts and experiences?

How can you become more involved in a range of professional development opportunities?

Take time to reflect. What are your next steps?

FIGURE 10.1   A baby engaged in a light box activity

Afterword

Thank you for taking the time to read my book and I hope you found it insightful.

I wanted to leave with a few final words for you to reflect upon as you leave my book of Being, Becoming and Thriving as an Early Years Practitioner.

I have taken you on a journey of being, becoming, and thriving. I have introduced you to the roots, shoots, and blooms of reflective questions, reflective accounts, and journal activities.

I now want you to imagine you have picked a dandelion, a dandelion that is at the stage of its life where it is no longer a round flower head. Instead, your dandelion has transformed into a plant with a large fluffy white seed head. Imagine holding your dandelion of hope and optimism and blow! Blow the seeds!

These seeds are your seeds of inspiration, reflection, strength, and resilience for what lies ahead for you in your studies and your career.

And remember, the only difference between a weed and a flower is judgement.

Annie

References

Ainsworth, M. D., Blehar, M. C., Waters, E., & Wall, S. (1978). Patterns of attachment: A psychological study of the strange situation. Hillsdale, NJ: Erlbaum.

Argyris, C. & Schon, D. (1978). *Organisational learning: A theory of action perspective.* Reading: Addison-Wesley.

Berlyne, D. E. (1960). *Conflict, arousal and curiosity.* New York: McGraw Hill.

Bowlby, J. (1969). *Attachment and loss.* Vol 1. New York: Basic Books.

British Educational Research Association. (2018) *Ethical guidelines for educational research* (4th ed.). https://www.bera.ac.uk/publication/ethical-guidelines-for-educational-research-2018.

Brookfield, S. (1994) *Becoming a critically reflective teacher.* San Francisco, CA: Jossey-Bass.

Brown, B. (2018). *Dare to lead.* London: Vermilion.

Bruce, T. (2011). *Early childhood education* (4th ed.). London: Taylor & Francis.

Bucknall, S. (2012). *Children as researchers in primary schools: Choice, voice, and participation.* Abingdon: Routledge.

Clarke, A. & Moss, P. (2011). *Listening to young children: The mosaic approach* (2nd ed.). London: National Children's Bureau.

Craft, A. (2000). *Creativity across the primary curriculum.* London: Routledge.

Early years foundation stage framework (2023). https://assets.publishing.service. gov.uk/media/65aa5e42ed27ca001327b2c7/EYFS_statutory_framework_for_ group_and_school_based_providers.pdf.

Equality Act (2010). https://www.gov.uk/guidance/equality-act-2010-guidance [Accessed 12th December 2022].

General Data Protection Act (2018). https://www.legislation.gov.uk/ukpga/2018/ 12/contents/enacted [Accessed 12 January 2023].

Gibbs, G. (1998). *Learning by doing: A guide to teaching and learning through reflective practice.* Oxford: Oxford Brookes University.

Goldschmied, E. & Jackson, S. (2004). *People under three: Children in day care.* Oxon: Routledge.

References

Hart, A. & Heaver, B. (2013). Evaluating resilience-based programs for schools using a systematic consultative review. *Journal of Child and Youth Development*, *1*(1), pp. 27–53.

Hart, R. A. (2013). *Children's participation: The theory and practice of involving young citizens in community development and environmental care*. Oxon: Routledge.

Maslow, A. H. (1943). Theory of human motivation. *Psychological Review*. *50*(4), pp. 370–396.

Pendrey, A. (2022). *The little book of reflective practice*. Oxon: Routledge.

Rogers, C. (1969). *Freedom to learn*. Columbus, OH: Charles E. Merrill Publishers.

Schon, D. A. (1983). *The reflective practitioner*. San Francisco, CA: Jossey-Bass.

United Nations Convention on the Rights of the Child (1989). https://www.unicef.org.uk/what-we-do/un-convention-child-rights/ [Accessed 3rd May 2022].

Glossary

Acronym Journal Activity Answers

- ADD – Attention Deficit Disorder
- ADHD – Attention Deficit Hyperactivity Disorder
- ASD – Autistic Spectrum Disorder
- CPD – Continuous Professional Development
- EHCP – Education Health Care Plan
- EP – Educational Psychologist
- ESOL – English for Speakers of a Second Language
- EYFS – Early Years Foundation Stage
- IBP – Individual Behaviour Plan
- IEP – Individual Education Plan
- NNEB – National Nursery Examination Board
- OFSTED – Office for Standards in Education, Children's Services and Skills
- PECS – Picture Exchange Communication System
- SENCO – Special Educational Needs Coordinator
- SEN – Special Educational Needs
- SLCN – Speech, Language and Communication Needs
- SpLD – Specific Learning Difficulty
- TAC – Team Around the Child
- VI – Visually Impaired

The inclusive practitioner personal core values many include the following:

- Loyal
- Intelligent
- Connection
- Creative
- Humane
- Respectful
- Diversity
- Generous
- Integrity
- Loving
- Open
- Religious
- Forgiving
- Faithful
- Wise
- Caring
- Honest
- Kindness
- Communicative
- Excellence
- Innovative
- Quality
- Inner strength
- Affectionate
- Courageous
- Professional
- Patient

Glossary

The inclusive practitioner professional core values many include the following:

- Honesty
- Integrity
- Loyalty
- Reflective
- Objective
- Accountability
- Reliable
- Discrete
- Inclusive
- Communicative
- Empathic
- Nurturer

Index

Index

Index

Printed in the United States
by Baker & Taylor Publisher Services